THE SONG OF SONGS

THE SONG OF SONGS

EDITED AS A DRAMATIC POEM

WITH INTRODUCTION, REVISED
TRANSLATION AND EXCURSUSES

BY

WILLIAM WALTER CANNON

Cambridge:
at the University Press
1913

CAMBRIDGE
UNIVERSITY PRESS

University Printing House, Cambridge CB2 8BS, United Kingdom

Published in the United States of America by Cambridge University Press, New York

Cambridge University Press is part of the University of Cambridge.

It furthers the University's mission by disseminating knowledge in the pursuit of
education, learning and research at the highest international levels of excellence.

www.cambridge.org
Information on this title: www.cambridge.org/9781107698055

© Cambridge University Press 1913

First published 1913
First paperback edition 2013

A catalogue record for this publication is available from the British Library

ISBN 978-1-107-69805-5 Paperback

PREFACE

SO much has been written about *The Song of Songs,* both in ancient and modern times, that any new writer may, not unreasonably, be asked to explain why he proposes to add to this large literature, and what he proposes to effect. My aim has been to write a little book for the use of those general readers who would like to have some knowledge of the subject, and who hardly know where to look for it. Some of the literature is not very easy of access, some is out of print, and some is not very attractive in form, or easy to use without close study. When I had spent some time on the study of this literature, it occurred to me that a short compilation from some of the best available sources might be of interest to many people who have not opportunity or leisure to quarry in libraries, or compare the contents of commentaries.

I have therefore written an *Introduction* in which I have endeavoured to give a concise account of such topics as are of interest to a student of the Song, and a discussion of those questions and theories on which there is difference of opinion, and the reasons which appear to me to justify my own views. Without a discussion of such questions it is impossible for a reader either to understand or appreciate the Song; and the consideration of them cannot be avoided. Where they appeared to be capable of general treatment I have inserted the discussion in the text, but where the question seemed to require a more technical treatment or an accumulation of details, I have thought it better to work it out in *Excursuses,* which I have put at the end of the book so that the reader need not be troubled with them unless he wishes.

I have added a *Revised Translation,* taking the Authorised Version as the basis. It seems almost sacrilege to lay hands on that lovely piece of English, and I have done my utmost not to spoil it. In this revision I have availed myself, as far as I could, of the fine poetical renderings of the late Prebendary Kingsbury in *The Speaker's Commentary*, which I have always admired, and which seem to me to be instinct with the spirit of the original.

Those readers who are already familiar with the subject will observe that I have not been able to adopt the modern views as to the interpretation of the poem propounded by Karl Budde and others. I trust that the careful examination of these views in my text will shew that they have not been rejected without due consideration, or without strong reasons being adduced why I cannot feel convinced by them. But the study of all alternative schemes has only strengthened my conviction, that the true interpretation is in the main that of Ewald, as modified by S. Oettli. Although I differ from the latter in some particulars, I consider his commentary, as a whole, by far the best of those I have consulted, and it has been of great use to me.

I am conscious that the aims which I set before myself when I planned this work were not easy to realise. I wish my readers not only to understand the Song, but to enjoy it. I have striven to bring out, as closely and yet as vividly as I could, its force and significance as a piece of ancient literature. That must be the primary aim of every editor. But I wish, even more, to impart to my readers some at least of the delight which I have felt in the study of this masterpiece of loveliness; some of the joy which caused its first editor to style it "the best Song of all." And I have also endeavoured to observe in my treatment of the subject the restraint and the reverence which ought to be the attitude of a writer who is treating, from any point of view, a portion of the Sacred Canon. If, notwithstanding the imperfections of the execution, I have to any extent achieved these aims, I may perhaps be justified in hoping that I have made a little contribution to Sacred Science. " In tabernaculo Dei offert unusquisque quod potest. Alii aurum, argentum, et lapides pretiosos, alii byssam, et purpuram, et coccum offerent, et hyacinthum. Nobiscum bene agetur si obtulerimus pelles et caprarum pilos " (Hieron. *Prologus Galeatus*).

I desire to express my most hearty thanks to Mr Norman McLean, M.A., Fellow of Christ's College, Cambridge, who has been good enough to read the whole of the proof-sheets, and (I need hardly add) has greatly improved the accuracy of the work. Those who are aware of the gigantic tasks in which Mr M°Lean is engaged will appreciate the extent of his kindness.

I desire equally to express my obligations to the Rev. Professor Sayce, Oxford, to whom, although personally unknown to him, I ventured to apply when I was in need of information. His prompt and courteous replies to my letters were of the greatest service to me, and I tender him my thanks.

I should be indeed ungrateful if I failed to express to the Governors of the John Rylands Library, Manchester, and to their Library Staff, my acknowledgments for the splendid hospitality they extend to students. Much of the preparation for this book has been made in that beautiful building, and I do not know how I could have accomplished it had I not had access to the valuable contents of its shelves. Only those who are able to use this Library know how valuable it is, and how courteous and helpful are those in charge of it.

Lastly, I should like to express my thanks to the Staff of the Cambridge University Press for the great care and pains spent on passing the sheets through the press.

W. W. CANNON

April 1913

TABLE OF CONTENTS

INTRODUCTION

1. SECULAR POETRY OF THE OLD TESTAMENT.

THE literature of the Old Testament is so predominantly religious, and everywhere so pervaded by religious influences, that peculiar interest must attach to those small portions of it of which the point of view is entirely secular. Especially this will be the case with regard to *poetry*. The religious poetry of the Hebrews is one of the most remarkable developments of their wonderful history, but this great truth should not be allowed to obscure the fact that they had also some poetry in which no religious interest can be discerned; and which dealt with the joys and sorrows, the interests and emotions of the secular life. Of the secular poems which have been preserved to us may be named:

The ancient song of vengeance. Gen. iv. 23 f.
The Well-digging song. Num. xxi. 17 f.
The ode of triumph over Heshbon. Num. xxi. 27 f.
David's great elegy over Saul and Jonathan. 2 Sam. i. 19 f.
and his short one over Abner. 2 Sam. iii. 33 f.

To these may be added some fragments or sayings:

Samson's riddle. Jud. xv. 16.
The song of David's triumphs. 1 Sam. xviii. 7.
The little song about Tyre. Is. xxiii. 16.

These valuable remains of a literature otherwise lost to us probably owe their preservation to the fact that they have a bearing on national history, and were preserved by historians as illustrative of the events they were narrating, like certain pieces in prose, such as the *mashal* of Jotham (Jud. ix. 7—16) or the speech of the wise woman of Abel (2 Sam. xx. 18).

But the *popular* poetry of Israel would be a blank had there not been handed down to us the beautiful poem, springing out of the very life of the people, which is named *The Song of Songs*. This exquisite production reveals to us that, while the poetic genius of the Hebrew nation soared to its highest flights in the expression of religious emotion, there were also poets capable of giving utterance in song to the most universal of all human emotions. The Sacred Canon abounds in writings which view the religious aspect of human life in manifold ways, but the reader may be thankful that one piece has been included which gives lyric expression to what has inspired poets in every age and every country. Old Testament literature would have been incomplete without this poem of *Human Love*[1].

2. Difficulties of interpretation of the Song.

Although it is evident that this poem deals with *love*, the love of man and woman, its interpretation presents extraordinary difficulties. No book in the Old Testament has given rise to a greater divergence of explanation. Whether this arises from the fact that there is no standard of comparison, because there is nothing at all like this book in Hebrew literature, or from the amount which in any view has to be read between the lines[2] if the poem is to be made intelligible at all, or from the too great ingenuity of theory which has been applied to it, there is no question as to the difficulty. Nor is this lessened by the very large amount of literature which has been devoted to the subject. The student is appalled by mountains of commentary in which every word and letter has been subjected to the most exhaustive examination with the most varying results—by theories supported by the profoundest erudition and the greatest acumen—and by illustrative matter collected with the greatest industry from every quarter. Nor can it be said that any view is so well established as to have obtained the unanimous suffrages of competent judges. The matter is still *sub judice*, and there is hardly any theory or principle of interpretation in support

---

[1] See v. Orelli in Schaff-Herz. *Enc.* art. *Song of Songs*.
[2] Driver, *Introd.* 1st ed. p. 411.

of which the powerful authority of eminent scholars could not be quoted. There is an interest, it may be said a fascination, in the subject, which perpetually incites to fresh effort. To everyone who is tempted once more to essay the difficult task of interpretation, the problem makes a fresh appeal. The labours of a long train of his predecessors lie before him— perchance while utilising their results he may avoid their extravagances. Perhaps he may be able to make some little contribution to a sound exegesis in the future, to lay a stone which may serve to support the solid edifice which the destined interpreter will some day build. Let us then adventure this daring quest and once more examine this enigmatical text: let us also make our endeavour to arrive at a theory of its interpretation. The field is open to all. It has been well observed that the proof of the soundness of such an attempt can only be such a degree of success in explanation as without solving every difficulty may on the whole recommend itself by simplicity and adherence to the text[1]. Simplicity indeed seems to be the quality most to be desired in such a task. The more elaborate and complicated the scheme of interpretation is, the more vulnerable it becomes, because it presents more points for attack. It will be the aim of the following pages to examine the principal questions which arise upon the text with regard to the various views which have been formed upon them, and to endeavour to extract from this mass of materials some conclusions which may not only render this ancient poem intelligible, but may also bring out its beauties and reveal its ethical purpose.

3. The Title prefixed to the Poem.

This poem has no title, the superscription i. 1 having been added at a later date. This is agreed by all commentators on the ground of the demonstrative pronoun made use of, which differs from that used throughout the poem[2].

---

[1] "Den einzig durchschlagenden Beweis für die Richtigkeit derselben kann selbstverständlich nur der gelungene Versuch leisten, die einheitliche Entwicklung der Handlung bis zu einem befriedigenden Abschlusse in einer Weise durchzuführen welche vielleicht im einzelnen wohl noch dunkle Stellen zurücklässt, im ganzen aber durch Einfachheit und textgemässe Auslegung sich empfiehlt." Oettli.

[2] אֲשֶׁר in the superscription, שֶׁ in the poem—see in Exc. III. post.

The expression "The Song of Songs" שִׁיר הַשִּׁירִים does not mean "a Song consisting of a number of Songs," nor can the whole phrase mean, "one of Solomon's many songs," with a reference to 1 Kings v. 12[1]. The expression *Song of Songs* is an ordinary Hebrew form of the superlative and means here "The best of all possible songs," "The finest poem of all poems[2]." The question of authorship will be dealt with in another place, but the above designation makes it clear that the author, whoever he might be, could not have written the superscription. No author, whatever his own opinion of the value of his production, could write on the title-page "The best of all songs." This title must rather be considered to be the verdict of a later age when the pre-eminent beauty of the Song was generally admitted.

The Targum, commenting on this title, observes, "Ten songs were uttered in this world. The best of all these was this one." The ten songs are then detailed.

"The first at the time when Adam received pardon for his guilt on the Sabbath day which came to shield him" (Psalm xcii).

The second the song of Moses (Ex. xv).

The third the song of the well (Num. xxi. 17).

The fourth the song of Moses (Deut. xxxii).

The fifth the song of Joshua when the sun and moon stood still (Jos. x. 12).

The sixth the song of Barak and Deborah (Jud. v).

The seventh the song of Hannah (1 Sam. ii).

The eighth David's song (2 Sam. xxii).

"The ninth song was sung by Solomon king of Israel by means of the Holy Spirit before the Lord, Sovereign of the Universe.

And the tenth song will once be sung by the children of the exile when they shall be redeemed from captivity" (see Is. xxx. 29)[3].

---

[1] Delitzsch, *Com.*, p. 18.

[2] Compare Gen. ix. 25, עֶבֶד עֲבָדִים, "the vilest slave," Exod. xxvi. 33, קֹדֶשׁ הַקֳּדָשִׁים, "the very holiest place," and many other examples, *Ges.-K.* 133. 3*i*.

[3] *The Targum to the Song of Songs*, trans. by H. Gollancz. Lusac and Co., 1909, pp. 7—9.

So Origen, in his First Homily on the Canticles, after enumerating the six songs in Exod. xv; Num. xxiv; Deut. xxxii; Jud. v; 2 Sam. xxii; Ps. xviii and Is. v, and remarking on each, proceeds "When thou shalt have passed through all, ascend yet higher, so that with reverent mind thou mayest be able with the bridegroom to sing also this Song of Songs[1]."

4. THE UNITY OF THE POEM.

The first question for consideration in regard to the Song is this: Is it one piece with a real internal unity, or a collection of unconnected fragments? The latter opinion was expressed by some of the older commentators, e.g. by Magnus (1842), who "could see in this book nothing else than a collection of various erotic pieces; some perfect, others imperfect, some amended, others interpolated, all the work of different authors and written in various ages[2]." This view, after being laid to rest for some time, was revived by Budde and Siegfried in a somewhat different form and has now many adherents. According to Budde the poem is "a bundle of love songs[3]," of which he counts twenty-three. Siegfried considers it "a collection of ten songs[4]." It is impossible to form any judgment upon the interpretation of this poem unless this very important question, as to whether it is an artistic whole or a mere mosaic of fragments, be first decided.

There are two ways of arriving at such a decision: (1) by examining the structure and language of the poem, (2) by ascertaining whether it reveals a connected story or argument running through it. It is proposed in this place to see what can be learned from its structure and its language[5].

---

[1] Quum universa transieris, ad altiora conscende ut possis anima decora cum sponso et hoc canere Canticum Canticorum (Interp. Hier. *Opp.*, ed. Vallarsi, 1735, III. p. 501). [2] Ginsburg, *Com.* p. 95.

[3] "An ein Bündel von Liebesliedern ist deshalb nach allen Anzeichen zuerst zu denken, nur diese Annahme vermag alle Erscheinungen zu erklären" (p. xvi).

[4] "So wie uns das Hohelied überliefert ist, lässt sich in demselben eine Sammlung von 10 Liedern bzw. Liederkränzen erkennen, deren einige verstümmelt oder glossiert sind" (p. 91).

[5] For much of what follows, see Oettli, *Com.*, p. 156 ; Bruston, *La Sulammite*, p. 10 f.

In the first place the poem is obviously framed on a plan. It is divided into five portions, the first four of which are closed by an adjuration to the daughters of Jerusalem, ii. 7, iii. 5, v. 8, viii. 4, each marking a pause in the movement or action of the poem. Although these four formulae are not exactly like each other they are so much so that it can hardly be doubted that they must have been designed to articulate the poem and form a framework on which to arrange the episodes, as well as in three instances, ii. 7, iii. 5, viii. 4, to point the moral of what has gone before, and to lead up to and prepare the reader for the great moral of the poem viii. 6, 7. It is equally obvious that such a formula was not necessary and would have been out of place at the end of the poem, viii. 14, and was therefore not inserted there. Such a deliberate construction of the poem cannot be fortuitous. It must be the result of a deliberate, thought-out scheme. The same poet must have written these four adjurations, and have written them to form the framework and to further the didactic and ethical purpose of his poem. The structure of the poem reveals its unity[1].

Turning to the language of the poem we find that while it is full of characteristic and most peculiar phrases and words, some of which are found nowhere else in Old Testament literature; these are distributed impartially over all parts of the poem, and persons and things mentioned casually in one place are mentioned equally casually in others. Thus:

The daughters of Jerusalem, i. 5; ii. 7; iii. 5, 10, 11; v. 8, 16; viii. 4.

Shulammite's brothers, i. 6; viii. 8.

Her mother, iii. 4; viii. 2, 5.

"My vineyard" [כרמי שלי] used figuratively, i. 6, viii. 12.

Keeping a vineyard [נטר], nowhere else in Old Testament, i. 6; viii. 11, 12.

"Whom my soul loves," i. 7; iii. 1—4.

The companions of the lover, i. 7; viii. 13.

The lover tending his flocks, i. 7; ii. 16; vi. 2, 3.

"O fairest among women," i. 8; v. 9; vi. 1.

---

[1] "Es ist *Einheit* in diesem Büchlein, denn es zeigt einen Gedankenforschritt in mehrfacher Richtung, und erst bei seiner Annahme sind alle Theile verständlich." König, *Einleit.* p. 422.

"My friend" [רעיתי], addressed to Shulamite, i. 9, 15; ii. 2, 10, 13; iv. 1, 7; v. 2; vi. 4.

Nard, i. 12; iv. 13, 14; nowhere else in Old Testament.

Henna-flower [כפר], i. 14; iv. 13; nowhere else in Old Testament.

"Thine eyes are doves," i. 15; iv. 1; v. 12.

"Sick with love," ii. 5; v. 8.

"O that his left hand were under my head and his right hand were embracing me," ii. 6; viii. 3.

The lover like a gazelle, ii. 9, 17; viii. 14.

"Fawn" [עפר], ii. 9, 17; iv. 5; vii. 4; viii. 14; nowhere else in Old Testament.

Grape-bloom [סמדר], ii. 13, 15; vii. 13; nowhere else in Old Testament.

"Let me hear thy voice," ii. 14; viii. 13.

Shulamite tends the vineyards, i. 6; ii. 15; vii. 13.

"He feeds his flock among the lilies," ii. 16; vi. 3.

"My beloved is mine and I am his," ii. 16; vi. 3; vii. 11.

"Till the day breathe and the shadows flee," ii. 17; iv. 6.

"Be like a gazelle *on the mountains*," ii. 17; viii. 14.

The two dream-scenes, iii. 1—4; v. 2—7.

The house of the mother, iii. 4; viii. 2, 5.

"Who is this coming up from the desert?" iii. 6; viii. 5.

Repetition of iv. 1—3, in vi. 5—7 with the word וּלְשֵׁי (meaning uncertain; nowhere else in Old Testament), iv. 1; vi. 5.

Two breasts—two fawns, iv. 5; vii. 4.

Caresses sweeter than wine, i. 2; iv. 16.

Precious things [מגדים], iv. 12, 16; vii. 14.

"My dove, my perfect one," v. 2; vi. 9.

Beds of balsam, v. 13 (reading עֲרוּגֹת), vi. 2.

The vine has sprouted, the pomegranates have flowered, vi. 11; vii. 13.

The neck compared to a tower, iv. 4; vii. 7.

The palate sweet, v. 16; vii. 10.

Shulamite in the garden, vi. 2, 11; vii. 13; viii. 13.

Caresses [דודים] i. 2, 4; iv. 10; v. 1; vii. 13.

שֶׁ all through.

It is equally important to notice that the other grammatical and linguistic peculiarities of the poem are equally to be found in every part of it[1]. Thus examples of the use of masculine for feminine forms of verbs are found, i. 6; ii. 5, 7; v. 8, 9; vii. 2. Examples of masculine for feminine pronouns are found, ii. 7; iv. 2; v. 4, 8; vi. 5, 8, and certain feminine forms do not appear in the poem at all, while the provincial and Aramaic forms are to be found in every part of the piece. The language of Canticles is admittedly so peculiar as to be unique, and it is all equally peculiar.

It is impossible to explain these phenomena satisfactorily, except on the assumption that the poem is one work of one author. Some of the minor peculiarities of grammar and diction might be explained on the theory that popular songs orally handed down would take the forms of speech current in the district where they were first committed to writing[2]. But such an explanation is quite inadequate to explain such phenomena as the structure of the poem and the very numerous and striking phrases found repeated in every part of it. And it must be remembered that they are repeated in a very limited space—the poem is only 116 verses long. The individuality of the author stands out in every part. Even if in any place he may be thought to have made use of existing materials (and this is not very likely) he must have rewritten them in his own language, filled them with his own striking locutions, and transfused them with his own genius. The poem tells us plainly, by facts apparent on the face of it, that it is not a song-cycle or *liederkranz* but an organic whole—that it is the product of one mind at one time—and that being a unity it must be studied and interpreted as a whole.

[1] See Excursus III.

[2] "Dann genügt zur Erklärung der Gleichartigkeit der Stücke, der gleiche Ort und die gleiche Zeit der Sammlung. Vielleicht längst überliefert, erscheinen Volkslieder im Volksmunde stets weitergebildet bis auf den Augenblick der Niederschrift und nehmen das Gewand der Gegend an, in der Mann den Fluss auffängt und fasst." Budde.

5. THE SONG A DRAMATIC POEM.

From the time of Origen onwards[1] it has been recognized by nearly all expositors of this poem that it is *dramatic*. The author does not, as in an epic poem, recount or describe in his own person the story or argument he wishes to set forth. The action of the poem is brought out by the agency of speakers who are introduced and characterised, so that, by what they say in various forms, the reader or auditor may be informed of the idea of the piece and the movement of the story. This may be done in various ways—by short ejaculatory speech, i. 4ᵃ; or longer speech, i. 5, 6, 12—14; ii. 3—8; iv. 1—7; vii. 2—10, &c.; by dialogue, i. 7, 8; i. 16—ii. 2; or by question and answer, v. 9—16; vi. 1, 2; viii. 13, 14. It may also be done by recounting past episodes, vi. 9—vii. 1; or dreams, iii. 1—5; v. 2—7; or by vividly describing episodes through the auditor or spectator, ii. 8—17; iii. 6—11; viii. 5ᵃ. In such ways as these the poet allows his characters to reveal his action and the argument has to be constructed by putting together the indications derived from these speeches, descriptions and narrations.

This feature of the poem is so marked that it cannot be effaced by any scheme of interpretation or theory of construction. Thus Graetz, who considers the whole poem to be one long monologue of the Shulamite, without any other speaker being introduced, is constrained to admit that there is a question and answer in v. 9, though he will not hear of any other dialogue.

So also those authors who consider the piece as a mere collection of songs bound together by an editor admit a "dramatic flavour" and some dramatic scenes[2], and certainly

---

[1] Dramatis in modum, et tanquam fabula quae in scenis personarum immutatione agi solet, videatur esse compositum.

Frequenter nos admonere convenit quod libellus hic in modum dramatis texitur. Prologus interp. Ruf. *Opp.* ed. De la Rue III. 26 E—78 c.

[2] "Ein dramatischer Beigeschmack entsteht ganz von selbst...selbst zu eigentlich dramatischen Auftritten kann sich dergleichen leicht steigern, nicht aber zu einem zusammenhängenden Drama." Budde.

"As a matter of fact Budde himself by the characteristics he assigns to the redactor points the way again past his own hypothesis to the dramatic view of the song." Rothstein, Hastings' *Bib. Dict.*, iv. 594.

anyone who is satisfied of the unity of the poem cannot feel any doubt that it is *a dramatic poem*.

A far more difficult question arises here which requires the most careful consideration. The question is whether this unquestionably dramatic poem is in fact a *drama* intended to be represented on a stage. A true solution of this question is vital to the interpretation of the poem. It is one thing to assign portions of a dramatic poem to the correct speakers, and to indicate the time, place, circumstances and conditions under which each speaks, or recounts or explains—who is thought to be present, or, whether present or absent, to be addressed or invoked—or what history of the past is related. It is quite another and a far more difficult enterprise to exhibit the whole piece in the model of a modern drama with acts and scenes, exits and entrances, stage directions and stage effects, and the whole *mise en scène* of a theatre of modern times as M. Bruston has done. If this ancient oriental poem is to be forced into such a mould, the difficulty of arriving at a satisfactory explanation of its peculiarities will be enormously increased, and it will be almost impossible to explain many of its most characteristic phenomena. Before therefore proceeding to an analysis of the poem, or any attempt to draw out the story it contains, we will first address ourselves to the question whether it may be reasonably supposed to have been intended for dramatic representation on the stage.

Ewald[1] assumes, on very slight grounds, that the Hebrews did possess the rudimentary beginnings of drama[2], and that Canticles although destined for a very simple stage yet relatively was very complete, and that no competent person could doubt that it was a stage play (*Spielstück*). He proceeds to point out that the principal characters are very few, and that this number has to be regulated by the capacity of the stage which the dramatist has at his disposal, so that he must handle his material and adjust the action with a view to this limited number of actors. Pointing to this peculiarity of the form, that often one person repeats the speeches of others as viii. 8—10; vi. 10—vii. 1, he asks why the poet adopts this plan of speech

---

[1] *Dichter*, ed. 1866, I. 1, p. 65 f.

[2] He considers רִאִי Nahum iii. 6 and עֵין Zach. v. 6 to have the meaning θέατρον, *Schaustück*.

within speech, scene within scene. Obviously, he says, the poet had to be economical with his characters; he could only put a few people on his stage at once, and so it was his plan for one person, if practicable, to imitate other voices and represent other scenes. So he considers that in Canticles less than three principal characters would be insufficient but that three would be enough—a maiden, a hero, a group of women[1]. Solomon is the hero for the great part of the drama; in the last act, where he falls out, the country friend of the maiden takes his place. The group of women may represent the palace ladies of Solomon, the women of Jerusalem, iii. 8—11, or country girls, viii. 5. It is enough, he says, to picture to oneself a simple stage of this kind where the two disputants (*streitende Seiten*) are represented each only by one person, and the chorus by two or three women. It would be more difficult to imagine these three personalities represented by only one actor, since the voices of all three are dissimilar. He then proceeds to divide the piece into five acts and thirteen songs, partly solos, partly duets (*Wechselgesänge*), and finally styles it a musical drama (*Singspiel*).

An even more peculiar arrangement is suggested by Renan[2] to explain how it is that the actors recount or describe rather than act, and that one reports the words of others. "When we seek to represent to ourselves the circumstances under which this singular drama was played, we are led to think of a platform where three principal actors figure—the shepherd, the shepherdess, and the king. The shepherdess is placed between the king and the shepherd, and in turns receives their homages. These actors are always present even at moments when according to stage conventions they ought to be absent. The actors express by their gestures and the expression of their features the sentiments which animate them (vi. 5). The meetings and, in one place (iv. 6—v. 1), the kiss of the two lovers, the fainting fits of the shepherdess falling into the arms of the shepherd, the delight of the shepherdess asleep supported on the arm of her beloved (viii. 5), and some other circumstances of this kind, were really represented, as the exclamations of the

---

[1] Origen thought there were "Quatuor personas, virum et sponsam—cum sponsa adolescentulas—cum sponso sodalium greges." De la Rue III. 12.

[2] *Le Cantique des Cantiques*, p. 78 f.

chorus or still more clear indications prove; but in detail there was no anxiety to present to the eyes a complete and possible action. Behind or around the three principal actors the secondary persons must have been arranged, forming two choruses, one of men, the other of women, who intervened in the piece with reflections suited to the occasion, and at times executed evolutions (iii. 6—11). The scene vi. 11—vii. 11 supposes dances or entertainments like our ballets! Some parts were undoubtedly sung." M. Renan did not think these entertainments took place in public, but supposed that they were represented at family gatherings (*des jeux privés et en famille*) and especially at wedding feasts.

More complicated still is the setting suggested by Oettli [1]. After pointing out the difficulty caused by the Shulamite speaking to her lover, i. 4, and recounting his words, ii. 8 f., and his speaking himself, iv. 8 f., on all which occasions he is invisible to the audience, Oettli remarks, "The poet puts aside the difficulty with a skilful hand in this way that he at the same time erects in the background of the present action a second stage, on which he permits the reader or spectator to cast a rapid informing (*orientirenden*) glance into the immediate past, which shews him the principal persons in such a relation to each other as illuminates the course and development of the main action with the brightness of lightning," and he compares this arrangement with the stage within a stage in *Hamlet*.

All this is very artificial and ingenious, but there does not seem to be any solid reason why our poem should be treated as in any sense a stage play—in fact there are very substantial reasons which may be adduced to the contrary [2]. These reasons may be divided into (*a*) those specially relating to Canticles, (*b*) those relating generally to the possibility of stage plays having ever existed in Jewish life.

(*a*) As Siegfried observes, this poem is too short for a stage play. It could be played in half an hour, many

---

[1] *Com.*, p. 158. We are not quite clear if Oettli is here describing actual stage machinery or is using a metaphor.

[2] See the discussions in Graetz, *Shir ha Shirim*, p. 10 f.; Siegfried, *Com.*, p. 82 f.; Delitzsch, *Com.*, Introd. pp. 8, 11.

scenes would occupy only half a minute, and the longest,
vii. 12—viii. 4, can be slowly read aloud in two minutes.
It is difficult to think that such stage preparations as have
been suggested would be utilised for so short a piece. It
is certainly strange also if this poem was really intended
for dramatic representation, however simple, that there should
be an entire absence of any stage directions. The names
of the speakers are not indicated, nor the places where the
action happens, nor the division of the scenes. This is not of
consequence in a poem, but it would be of importance in an
acting play. Then again the construction of the piece is as
suited to a dramatic poem as it is unsuited to a stage play.
The phenomenon to which Ewald, Renan and Oettli call attention, the repeating of other people's speeches, the recounting of
events, the speaking to persons who are absent, would be
extremely tiresome on the stage, and the arrangements these
writers suggest to make it possible to act the piece, shew of
themselves that it was not written to be acted. The essence of
a stage play is *action*, developing a story by events, not by
recounting events. In a play intended to be acted the procession iii. 6—11 would not be described by a spectator, it
would march across the stage. The event vi. 11 f. would not
be recounted, but enacted. A stage writer would show the
moving scene viii. 5ᵃ, and not let a spectator relate it. And
surely the beloved whose voice we hear ii. 8 f. and iv. 8 f.
would be on the stage and not out of sight. The fact is that
the piece, though intensely *dramatic*, is not *scenic* and is not
meant to be.

And if we accept the early date of this poem any idea of a
stage play at that period becomes absolutely startling. We
should have to assume a theatrical system in Israel 300 years
earlier than Thespis and nearly 1000 before the first known
Indian drama. Is this credible?

(b) But there is no reason to think that there ever was
a Jewish drama, or that the nation of Israel from the beginning
to the end of its career ever shewed any inclination to dramatic
composition, or had any feeling or understanding for stage-
craft. All the literature of the Old Testament, even that
which is not distinctively religious in its aim and scope, is
written with an ethical tendency. There is no trace in all this

literature of anything written merely for amusement or diversion, and there failed altogether in the Hebrew character those elements of detachment and simple joy in life, as well as the mythological system, which in the Hellenic race produced the drama. There is not an allusion in all that literature which gives any colour to the idea of a stage play having ever been acted in Israel. The *dialogue* exists not only in the book of Job but in the prophets (cf. Is. xxi. 6—10, 11; Mic. vi. 6—8), but there is no hint of scenic representation. There is in fact evidence of a late date which shews clearly how the religious side of Judaism felt toward the drama. About 173 B.C. Jason and Menelaus incurred the hatred of the pious by informing Antiochus Epiphanes "that they were desirous to leave the laws of their country and the Jewish way of living and to follow the King's laws and the Grecian way of living," and they obtained royal protection for the erection of gymnasia and the performance of other Greek games[1]. But the first theatre in Jerusalem was erected by Herod the Great, as also a great amphitheatre in the plain. "Both of them were indeed admirable and costly works but opposite to the Jewish customs, for we have had no such shows delivered to us as fit to be used or exhibited by us[2]." It is difficult to think that this strong objection would have been felt if the performance of stage plays had been an ancient institution in Israel.

It cannot then be considered proved or even likely that Canticles was written for the stage or performed upon it—and this conclusion will, it is conceived, remove many difficulties which the stage theory has caused in interpreting the poem. There is so much more liberty of movement about a dramatic poem. The author is not concerned about entries and exits and who is on the stage. If he wants a character, he can produce him without a formal entry, and when he wants him no more as iii. 11, or iv. 7, no formal exit is required. Writing in a series of pictures it is natural that he should allow any speaker to recount speeches or events. The voice in iv. 8 might be a difficulty on the stage, it is none in the poem. The poet can see the speaker. Nor is he bound to any unity of time or developing

---

[1] Joseph. *Ant.* XII. 5. 1. See the horrified comments in 1 Macc. i. 11—15, 2 Macc. iv. 13—17.

[2] Joseph. *Ant.* XV. 8. 1.

progress of action. He may put in his pictures where he likes, and vi. 11 may be logically the introduction to i. 4[a] and viii. 8, 9 to i. 6[b], provided in the result all necessary matters are introduced. Remove the idea of stage representation and none of those violent dislocations will be required which some interpreters have so freely indulged in[1]. An allusion in one place will recall a narration in another.

When carefully examined most of the elaborate polemic of late levelled against the *dramatic unity* of the poem is really directed against the *stage theory*. Remove that, and most of these criticisms fall to the ground[2]. The writer believes that if the work is viewed in the right light as a dramatic poem, and freed from these stage preconceptions, it will be found as capable of rational interpretation as the dramatic poems of Robert Browning which, though written in our own day and our own language, have not always been considered to be so clear as to obviate some difference of opinion as to their meaning.

From the form of the poem it would seem to have been designed to be sung or recited on festive occasions. It is known that it was customary among the richer classes to enliven their feasts with music (Am. vi. 5, Is. v. 12, xxiv. 9), and one may well imagine this poem either sung on such occasions, or recited by a skilled performer who, by varied voice and gesture, indicated its movement and story. The title given to the piece, its preservation and its ultimate reception into the Sacred Canon, make it certain that it was not only well known, but widely appreciated as a treasure of national literature.

6. THE PERSONS OF THE POEM.

Having arrived at the conclusion that this poem is a *unity*, and that it is *dramatic* in character we may now proceed to examine who are the persons represented in it. There is no direct indication in the piece itself of the persons to whom the various speeches or narrations are to be assigned, although in

---

[1] See Excursus II., and for a very fantastic rearrangement see *Das Hohe Lied*, K. Kohler, Chicago, 1878.

[2] See Rothstein, *Das Hohe Lied*, 1893, p. 6.

most cases there is not really much difficulty in ascertaining the speakers. In many Greek MSS. an attempt is made to supply this deficiency though without much real help being given to the interpreter, as they generally follow the exegesis of Origen and divide the speeches between his four characters[1]. The most detailed and interesting of these attempts is found in the Codex Sinaiticus (ℵ), where they are inserted in red ink in the text. Some of these are very striking, especially where they contain a trace of the allegorical interpretation, as before i. 7 the rubric reads "To Christ the bridegroom[2]," and before the words in iv. 16, "Let my beloved come," is inserted "The bride asks the Father that the bridegroom may come down[2]." But the fact that these rubrics are so closely bound up with the system of interpretation which prevailed in the Christian Church after Origen, renders them of little or no value, and we shall be obliged to rely on the indications furnished by the text itself.

This text reveals these characters: (1) a maiden whose name is not given but who is described as "the Shulamite" (vii. 1), "the girl from Shulem or Shunem" (they are the same place). She pervades the whole piece, and is present as far as we can see in every scene; (2) King Solomon, sometimes called only "the King," i. 4, 12, vii. 6; sometimes by his name, i. 5; iii. 7, 9, 11; viii. 11, 12; (3) another character—a man—spoken of as "my beloved," i. 12, 14, 16; ii. 3, 8, 9, 10, 16, 17; iv. 16; v. 2, 4, 5, 6, 8, 9, 10, 16; vi. 1, 2, 3; vii. 11, 12, 14; viii. 5, 14; or as "He whom my soul loves," i. 7, iii. 1, 3, 4, and who is also spoken of as a shepherd, i. 7; ii. 16; vi. 3; (4) a group of ladies called "the daughters of Jerusalem," i. 5; ii. 7; iii. 5, 10, 11; v. 8, 16; viii. 4. Beyond these there do not seem to be any speaking characters; the descriptions in iii. 6—11 and viii. 5ᵃ may well be ascribed to the poet himself and the words of other persons, vi. 10, viii. 8—10, are recounted, by some one of the speaking persons.

Much help will be gained in interpretation if it is observed how carefully the characters are distinguished in the epithets

---

[1] See footnote 1, p. 11, sup. and Riedel, *Die Auslegung des H. L.*, 106—9.

[2] i. 7 απαγγειλον (pr. προς τον νυμφιον χν̄), iv. 16 καταβητω (pr. η νυμφη αιτειται τον πρᾱ ινα καταβη ο νυμφιος αυτου). See Swete's Sept. ad loc.

applied by them to each other[1]. When the Shulamite addresses her shepherd friend or speaks of him he is designated
as "my beloved," דּוֹדִי, or "whom my soul loves," שֶׁאָהֲבָה נַפְשִׁי,
sometimes with an allusion to his occupation as a shepherd.
When the daughters of Jerusalem speak of him, v. 9, vi. 1,
they use the same phrase, "thy beloved," דּוֹדֵךְ. When these
"daughters" address the Shulamite their address is always,
"O fairest among women," הַיָּפָה בַּנָּשִׁים. Solomon usually calls
the Shulamite "my friend," רַעְיָתִי, seven times; once only he
uses a little warmer term, "my dove, my perfect one," vi. 9.
The beloved alone, in a moment of the highest ecstasy, iv. 8—v. 1,
uses the striking phrase[2] "my sister betrothed," אֲחֹתִי כַלָּה or
simply "betrothed," and never uses "my friend" alone without
some other endearing epithet. Such careful characterisation
cannot be accidental, it must be deliberate, and be designed to
assist the reader or auditor to make out which of the characters
is speaking—and of whom—as well as to give light as to their
qualities and dispositions, and the part they are to play in the
development of the story.

    And who can help feeling the difference between the speeches
ascribed respectively to the king and to the shepherd? The frigid
flatteries of the earlier speeches, i. 9, 11; iv. 1—7; vi. 4—10 (with
passages repeated one from the other), rise indeed to a warmth
which is disagreeable in vii. 8, 9, but never speak the language
of pure and genuine love. They are largely descriptions of
physical beauty with no thought of moral qualities or the
beauties of character. The attempt to win affection by bribery,
i. 11, and the praise of this country girl as superior in beauty to
all the ladies of the royal harem, vi. 8, 9, leave us very cold;
one feels that these speeches have done duty before, and have
no meaning except to lead up to such a climax as is indicated
in vii. 9. Their best commentary is 1 Kings xi. 1.

    On the other hand there is no mistaking the genuine quality
of the fine passage iv. 8—15. This is pure affection directed,
not only to physical beauty, but also to higher qualities. This

---

[1] See Ewald, *Dichter* II. 343 f.

[2] The Egyptian analogies to this phrase referred to by Budde, p. xvi., seem
not to amount to much, since in Egypt the marriage of a brother to a sister was
quite common. See G. Maspero, *Les Contes populaires de l'Egypte ancienne.*
Paris, 1882, pp. 51—54 and n. p. 52.

lover can admire beautiful and appropriate speech, *v.* 11. He thinks of the virtuous maiden as a locked garden, a sealed fountain, a well of pure spring water, ice-cold streams from Lebanon. At the height of his passion he respects his betrothed, and shews himself worthy of her. His admiration of her physical beauty is expressed under the delicate metaphor of a garden of fragrant plants exhaling spicy odours. All is real and vivid, but nothing is gross. The contrast between this speech and those ascribed to Solomon is as marked as it well could be.

All this careful discrimination of characters ought to be of real help to us as we proceed to construct the argument and course of the story.

7. THE ARGUMENT OF THE POEM.

We are now in a position to reconstruct from indications contained in the poem itself the story which lies behind it and on the basis of which it develops its action.

The little town of Shunem or Shulem in the tribe of Issachar (Josh. xix. 18) and five miles from Mt Tabor (Jud. iv. 14), lying among the mountains which overlook the fruitful plain of Jezreel, was the home of the heroine, the "girl from Shulem," vii. 1. To the north and east the roads lead to the Galilean mountain region full of variegated charms, to the lordly Tabor, and to the beautiful shores of the lake of Gennesareth. South and west the prospect extends over the once richly cultivated highland of Ephraim and the noble wooded headland of Carmel, vii. 6, falling into the Western Sea. Not far away at Baal Hamon[1], King Solomon had a large and profitable vineyard, viii. 11. In this little town of Shulem lived a family comprising a mother, vi. 9, viii. 2, an only daughter, vi. 9, and two brothers, i. 6, viii. 8. The father is not mentioned and presumably was dead as the brothers appear as the natural guardians of their sister, viii. 8[2]. The family were possessors of vineyards and gardens, i. 6; vi. 10; viii. 2. The girl was remarkable for beauty and grace and possessed a fine voice,

---

[1] See Judith viii. 3 ἐν τῷ ἀγρῷ τῷ ἀνὰ μέσον Δωθάειμ καὶ Βαλαμών. See iv. 4.
[2] See, as to the position of brothers, Gen. xxxiv. 7 f.

ii. 14; viii. 13; comp. iv. 11. She had won and returned the love of a young farmer living not far away, the possessor of flocks of sheep, i. 7, 8, and of gardens, vi. 1—3. Their first happy meeting had taken place under an apple tree not far from the girl's home, viii. 5 [1], comp. ii. 3, and joyful meetings had taken place under overarching trees, i. 17, and at other pleasant places of resort, ii. 4. The relation had been a happy and a pure one: he calls her "sister betrothed," iv. 12, she thinks of him as "like a brother," viii. 1. The brothers, however, anxious for their sister's honour, and disliking a relation somewhat opposed to Oriental strictness in such matters, viii. 8, 9, sent her away from home to be a watcher in the vineyards, i. 6. The time was the early spring, ii. 11 f.; vi. 11; vii. 13 f., and she had been long enough in this employment to be scorched by the sun, i. 5; one day she had gone down to the nut-garden to observe the new growths of the spring, when her attention was caught by a glittering train, "the chariots of a prince's retinue," vi. 11, 12, namely, King Solomon [2], with a large number of the ladies of his court, vi. 8. These ladies saw and admired the country beauty, vi. 9, 10; she wished to withdraw but was called back by the admiring ladies, vii. 1. What happened next is not told except in its unhappy sequel, "The king has brought me into his apartments," i. 4 [3], and it is there we find her as the poem opens, longing to run away, ib.

It will be seen that the poet presents here a most interesting complication to be unravelled in his poem. The king is set against the young farmer. Will the majesty of the king, the glory of his surroundings, his presents, and his flattering persuasions, and the praises of his court ladies prevail against this country girl, or will she be able to resist these allurements and remain faithful to him whom her soul loves? Will her country lover have the devotion and courage to follow her to Jerusalem, seek out where she is detained, and find an

---

[1] The pointing in this verse must be corrected, and all the suff. read as fem. So Del. and nearly all commentators.

[2] Probably on his way to or from his "pleasaunce" in Lebanon, 1 Kings ix. 19. Ewald, *Gesch. E. T.* III. 257.

[3] Siegfried asks "woraus ersehen wir denn, dass wir uns überhaupt in einem Harem befinden? Das ist die *fable convenue.*" We can only reply that this is the plain meaning of the words i. 4, and that they have to be allegorised away to make them mean anything else.

opportunity of strengthening her resistance and animating her courage? Is the end to be that the Shulamite girl is to become one of the "innumerable girls," vi. 8, i. 3, in a royal harem, or the honourable wife of a farmer in Galilee? The poet makes us feel that a moral issue is involved, and prepares us to follow with the liveliest sympathy the fate of the pure girl, vi. 9, in her struggle against overwhelming odds.

Before however proceeding to analyse the various scenes of the poem in detail, on the basis of the argument as above set out, it will be necessary to examine two other theories of its scope and meaning, both of which have at various times received considerable support.

8. THE TRADITIONAL THEORY.

The oldest theory, on which was based all the allegorical exposition of the Christian Church, admitted only two principal characters, thus identifying Solomon and the beloved shepherd. In this view the poem describes the progress of the mutual affection of the two characters and their subsequent marriage, Solomon being at once the King, the Shepherd and the spouse[1]. This view, which until the eighteenth century was universally held, and which produced an enormous literature of commentary, is now mainly represented by Franz Delitzsch[2], whose abundant learning and fine feeling render his works indispensable to any serious student. If the theory is capable of being maintained at all, we may be sure that it will be set forth in its most attractive light by this prince of expositors, and the following statement of it is based almost entirely upon his commentary.

"Shulamith is a historic personage, a country maiden of humble rank who by her beauty and the purity of her soul filled Solomon with a love for her which drew him away from the

---

[1] So Origen, " ostenditur autem per haec quia sponsus hic etiam pastor fit." De la Rue III. 54 B.

[2] Com., Eng. Trans. 1891. Kingsbury (in the *Speaker's Commentary*) is based on Delitzsch, and the view of v. Orelli is not quite the same. " It is an art poem, perhaps composed for the celebration of some definite marriage, the composer of which represented the groom as Solomon and the bride as the Shulamite." Art. *Song of Songs* in Schaff.-Herz. *Enc.*

wantonness of polygamy, and made for him the primitive idea of marriage (Gen. iii. 23) a self-experienced reality. This sunny glimpse of paradisaical love, which Solomon experienced, again became darkened by the insatiableness of passion, but the Song has preserved it. Solomon appears here in loving fellowship with a woman such as he had not found among a thousand (Eccl. vii. 28), and although in social rank far beneath him he raises her to an equality with himself. That which attached her to him is not her personal beauty alone, but her beauty animated by nobility of soul. Solomon raises this child to the rank of queen, and becomes besides this queen as a child. The simple one teaches the wise man simplicity: the humble draws the King down to her level: the pure accustoms the impetuous to self-restraint. Following her, he willingly exchanges the bustle and outward splendour of court life for rural simplicity, wanders gladly over mountain and meadow if he only has her, with her he is content to live in a lowly cottage. The erotic external side of the poem has thus an ethical background." Following out this general idea Delitzsch divides and arranges the poem as follows.

FIRST ACT.

The mutual affection of the Lovers, i. 2—ii. 7.

In the Palace.

SCENE 1. vv. 2—8. Shulamite and Court ladies.

[The allusion to the shepherd, v. 7, 8, is thus explained: "The country damsel has no idea of the occupation of a king. Her simplicity goes not beyond the calling of a shepherd as of the fairest and the highest. She thinks of the shepherd of the people as the shepherd of sheep."]

The King enters.

SCENE 2. v. 9—ii. 7. Shulamite and the king. At the end she falls into a love ecstasy. Solomon supports and bears her up.

[v. 17 is thus explained, "The city with its noisy display does not please her. She knows indeed that her lover is a king, but she thinks of him as a shepherd. Therefore she praises the fresh green of their future homestead."]

SECOND ACT.

The mutual seeking and finding of the lovers, ii. 8—iii. 5.

At Shulamite's Home.

SCENE 1. ii. *vv.* 8—17. Monologue by Shulamite describes how Solomon visited her in her mountain home; she sang him a song of the vineyard and invited him to come again in the evening.

[*v.* 17 is thus explained, "She represents (Solomon) to herself as a shepherd, but in such a manner that, at the same time, she describes his actions in language which rises above ordinary shepherd life, and, so to speak, idealises. She, who was herself a shepherdess, knows from her own circle of thought nothing more lovely or more honourable to conceive and say of him than that he is a shepherd who feeds among lilies."]

SCENE 2. iii. 1—5. Shulamite's dream.

THIRD ACT.

The bringing of the bride and the marriage, iii. 6—v. i.

At Jerusalem.

SCENE 1. iii. *vv.* 6—11. Describes a procession with a bodyguard conveying Shulamite in a litter to the palace. Solomon shews himself to the object of his love and the jubilant crowd.

SCENE 2. iv. 1—v. 1. In the palace hall. Conversations between Solomon and Shulamite.

The wedding is supposed to take place between iv. 16 and v. 1.

FOURTH ACT.

Love disdained and won again, v. 2—vi. 9.

At Jerusalem.

SCENE 1. (*a*) Shulamite's dream, v. 2—8.

[The griefs and sad issue of this dream as opposed to the joyful ending of the first dream (iii. 1—5) are explained to rest on the fact that Shulamite had become estranged from the king. "She had lost her first love." "She is unwilling for his sake to put herself to trouble or to do that which is disagreeable to her." "She relates it with sorrow: for scarcely had she rejected him with these unworthy deceitful pretences when she comes to herself again[1]."]

(b) v. 9—vi. 3. Shulamite and Court ladies.

Solomon enters.

SCENE 2. vi. 4—9. Solomon speaks.

[On v. 8 it is remarked, "we conclude from these low numbers (!) that the Song celebrates a love-relation of Solomon's at the commencement of his reign."]

FIFTH ACT.

Shulamith the attractively fair but humble princess, vi. 10—viii. 4.

In Solomon's Park at Etam (Jud. xv. 8; Jos. *Ant.* VIII. 7. 3).

SCENE 1. (a) vi. 10—13. Shulamite and Court ladies.

[It is explained that wandering in the garden she met the Court ladies. "Amidst this her quiet delight in contemplating vegetable life, she had almost forgotten the position to which she had been elevated[2]."]

And on v. 12, "She places her joy in the loneliness of nature, in contrast to her driving along in a splendid chariot."]

Shulamite dances as requested, vii. 1[b].

(b) vii. 1—6. Court ladies.

SCENE 2. vii. 7—viii. 4. Solomon and Shulamite.

[On vii. 12 it is explained that "her simple childlike disposition longs for the quietness and plainness of rural life, away from the bustle and display of city and Court life," and on viii. 1, "Resigning herself now dreamily to the idea that

---

[1] So Kingsbury, "A transient cloud of doubt or estrangement is now passing over her soul, as by the relation of this dream she intimates to her friends. She has lost the society of the Beloved but not his affection, and seeks reunion with him."

[2] "She appears throughout, in the midst of courtly praise and honour, somewhat in the position of an exile longing to revisit her home." Kingsbury.

Solomon is her brother, whom she may freely and openly kiss, and her teacher besides, with whom she may sit in confidential intercourse under her mother's eye, she feels herself as if closely embraced by him."]

SIXTH ACT.

The Ratification of the covenant of love in Shulamith's native home, viii. 5—14.

SCENE 1. viii. 5, 7. Solomon and Shulamite, travelling to her mother's house.

["The loving pair as they wander arm in arm through the green pasture-land between Jezreel and Shunem till they reach the environs of the paternal home, which reminds them of the commencement of their love relations."]

SCENE 2. *vv.* 8—14. Shulamite, her brothers and Solomon.

[On *v.* 14 it is explained, "With this song breaking forth in the joy of love and life, the poet represents the loving couple as disappearing over the flowery hills[1]."]

Such in brief is the outline of Delitzsch's scheme, though, to do it justice, his commentary ought to be read at length. And, even displayed in its most attractive form, this theory does not convince; and its adherents at the present day are but few. In fact when the poem is carefully examined the objections to this method of interpretation are too strong to be resisted. They may be briefly summarised as follows[2]:

(*a*) This scheme of explanation takes away from the poem most of its interest and significance, by depriving it of any progress in its action or complication in its incidents. The lovers are met by no hindrance, and confronted by no difficulty. The marriage takes place iv. 16—v. 1, and all the slight action of the piece, and such movement and interest as it has, really comes to an end. Certainly all which follows from v. 2 to viii. 4 might be left out without loss—it leads to nothing. The supposed estrangement in the Fourth Act is too slight

---

[1] " She no longer thinks of the possibility of separation......His haunts and hers are henceforth the same." Kingsbury.

[2] See Driver's Introd.; Oettli, *Com.*, p. 157; Bruston, pp. 19—21.

and transient to rouse any interest and has no consequences, and the solitary ramble of the royal bride in the nut-garden and the explanation given of it, have no bearing on anything. On this theory the powerful adjuration three times repeated not to rouse prematurely the sentiment of love, ii. 7, iii. 5, viii. 4, has absolutely no force at all. The earnest aspiration after the presence of the beloved, i. 7, and the scornful answer lose all their force and become mere trifling. The resemblances and differences of the two dreams, iii. 1—4, v. 2—7, conceived on a most delicate psychological basis[1], lose all their meaning, although they must be the result of conscious art. The great culminating truth,

> If a man should give all the wealth of his house for love
> Men would surely despise him (viii. 7),

is of no force as a moral for this story, and the later part of the poem is only intelligible on the assumption that the heroine is not yet married. Can it be imagined that a husband would address to his happy young bride the language vii. 8—10? Again a young wife would hardly desire to take her husband to her mother's house "like a brother," viii. 1, 2. *His* house would be her home[2]. And finally the passage, viii. 10,

> I was a wall and my breasts like towers ;
> Then I was in his eyes like one who finds peace.

If this is to have any force at all it denotes successful resistance. How could it be applied to a young married woman?

(b) The Hebrew tradition of "Solomon in all his glory" represents him as magnificent in his tastes, loving a stately pomp and ceremony, surrounded by a numerous attendance of courtiers and a gorgeous equipment (see iii. 6—11). It is hard to think that a Hebrew poet would represent him not only as masquerading as a shepherd, i. 7, vi. 2, with a woodland home, i. 16, 17, ii. 6, but also as visiting a country girl in Galilee at her house in the early morning, ii. 8—17, and skipping over the hills like a gazelle, v. 9, and as a person whom she can think of taking to her mother's house, iii. 4, viii. 2. It is still harder to conceive that he thought of the lordly Solomon strolling with his bride through the country, lodging in the villages,

---

[1] See Budde, *Com.*, pp. 27—8.
[2] See iii. 4, and Siegfried's note.

visiting with interest the vineyards, and appearing in Shulem with his bride on his arm to take up his residence at her mother's house, vii. 12—viii. 5. Every reader would remember that at this time the king had been married sixty times, and had a large harem as well, vi. 8. Such adventures would be inconceivable to such a king at such a period; our poet could not have meant this. As Graetz pointed out, his aim was to establish strong contrasts. The *shepherd* skips over the hills, ii. 9, viii. 14. The *king* is carried in a palanquin, iii. 6—11. The *shepherd* has only one pure love, iv. 12; the *king* a large harem, vi. 10.

(c) But a far weightier objection to the traditional theory is that it takes from the poem its fine moral and its ethical character. It is revolting to the feelings to think that the Shulamite, a paragon of beauty and virtue, should willingly enter a harem of "sixty queens, eighty concubines and innumerable girls." How opposed is such a possibility to the moral of the poem in viii. 6—7. How could such a one as Solomon be thought to offer anything which resembled *love* as there so finely delineated, and how can such a relation be called *marriage* in any sense? As far as we can learn from the evidence of this poem and 1 Kings xi. 1—3, the only persons whom Solomon could be said to have married were foreign princesses, daughters of royal houses[1]. The other ladies of the harem are not "queens," they have inferior designations. A country girl from Galilee would merely be one of the עֲלָמוֹת, the numberless girls, vi. 8, who love Solomon, i. 3. In fact there is no marriage in this poem, only the hope and anticipation of one, v. 1. Solomon never speaks of marriage but merely of enjoyment and physical charms. There is nothing either pleasing or moral about the only relation that was possible between this king and this farmer's daughter. "What," remarks Oettli, "became of Shulamite afterwards?

---

[1] In the passage in Kings, Solomon's *wives* are described as נָשִׁים נָכְרִיּוֹת *v.* 1, and נָשִׁים שָׂרוֹת *v.* 3. These would be the same as the מְלָכוֹת in Cant. (the number in Kings is incredible, and no doubt Cant. has the earlier and sounder tradition); LXX. *v.* 3 γυναῖκες ἄρχουσαι. In 2 Chron. xi. 21 Rehoboam's *wives* נָשִׁים are similarly distinguished from פִּילַגְשִׁים, LXX. γυναῖκας and παλλακάς.

A poor deserted and neglected denizen of a harem, a satire on
viii. 7 f. No one in the whole history of Israel is less suited
than Solomon to represent in himself the mystery of wedded
love." We must not think of a happy married life in a cottage
at Shulem, but rather of something like the terrible picture in
Esther ii. 11 f. An interpretation which leads to such results
is self-condemned. The poet had a high and noble ideal of
love. When he wrote his great eulogy of it, he could not have
thought of mere sensuous passion whose sad result would be to
leave his lovely heroine in Solomon's harem, while the king
passed on to fresh conquests.

(d) Nor can we find in this poem or in the traditions in
Kings any trace of the supposed "conversion" of Solomon.
The suggested "estrangement" in the Fourth Act and the style
of language used by the king in ch. vii. shew that the author
did not attribute to him any moral elevation[1], and to the author
of Kings his later life was one of progressive deterioration.
It was in his later years that he introduced and patronised in
Jerusalem the licentious rites of the Phoenician Astarte and
incurred the hostility of the prophets, 1 Kings xi. 33, and so far
from thinking of him as an improved man, our poet obviously
despises him, viii. 7. Surveying these difficulties, we feel that
this interpretation is impossible, in fact it is now almost universally given up, and it is not likely that any new editor will
revive it. It is not without some regret that we feel bound to
sever ourselves from a theory which has been precious to
Christian expositors, which has enriched the meditations of
saintly mystics and brightened the strains of holy songs. Perhaps, however, some recompense for these losses may be found
in the consideration that the poem, as interpreted in our later
pages, furnishes a most powerful ethical example and displays
a moral which fully justifies its position in the Canon of Holy
Scripture.

We shall return to this subject on a later page, but at
present our attention is claimed by another theory of interpretation of much more modern date and of a widely different
character.

---

[1] So in the late tradition in Eccl. ii. 8 the king merely thinks of women as
possessions. "I provided for myself...the joys of the sons of men, a multitude
of women " שָׁדָּה וְשִׁדּוֹת. Volck's *Com.*

9. THE SYRIAN WEDDING THEORY.

This theory is based upon observations of marriage customs of a Syrian tribe, "a branch of the Soleb," living to the north of Damascus, made in 1861 by Dr J. G. Wetzstein, a man profoundly versed in the life of Syria at the present day[1]. The following quotations will give some idea of the important points.

1. "The fairest period in the life of a Syrian peasant are the first seven days after his marriage, in which, along with his young wife, he plays the part of king (*melik*), and she of queen (*melika*), and both are treated and served as such in their own district and by the neighbouring communities. The greater village weddings take place for the most part in the month of March, the most beautiful month of the Syrian year. ...Since the winter rains are past and the sun now refreshes and revives, and does not, as in the following months, oppress by its heat, weddings are celebrated in the open air on the village threshing-floor, which at this time of year, with few exceptions, is a flowery meadow."

2. "We pass over the wedding day itself, with its pomp, the sword-dance of the bride, and the great banquet. Bride and bridegroom awake on the morrow as king and queen. Already before sunrise they receive the leader of the bridesmen (now their vizier) and his men: they fetch the corn-drag[2] and bring it to the threshing-floor, singing a rousing song, the subject of which is Love or Warfare, generally both together. There it is erected as a throne and, after the royal pair have taken their seats and the necessary formalities are disposed of, begins a great dance in honour of the young pair. The accompanying song occupies itself entirely with them, and the unavoidable *wasf*, *i.e.* a description of the bodily perfection of both and of their ornaments, forms its main contents. The song is more restrained in praise of the queen, and praises her

---

[1] See App. to Del. *Com.*, Eng. Trans., 1891, pp. 162 f.; also Introds. to Budde's and Siegfried's *Commentaries*.

[2] *Dreschtafel*, made of boards bent upwards in front like a sledge and set with stones of porous basalt like teeth in rows, used to thrash the grain and chop the straw. This seems to be the same thing as the Heb. מוֹרַג, Is. xli. 15; 2 Sam. xxiv. 22; 1 Chr. xxi. 23.

visible rather than her hidden charms, because she is now a married woman and because the *wasf* which was sung to her yesterday during her sword-dance left nothing to be desired on this topic. This *wasf* is to our taste the weak point of the Syrian wedding songs, we find its similes often very clumsy, and discern all through stock forms....With this dance begin the games, which last seven days: they begin on the first day in the morning, on the others shortly before noon, and always last deep into the night, with lit fires: only on the last day all ends before sunset. During this whole week their two majesties are dressed in wedding garb, may do no work, and care for nothing; they have only to look down from the *merteba* (throne) on to the games played before them, in which they themselves only take a moderate part. The queen dances more frequently to let her bridal ornaments be admired."

This description, and other details which will be considered later, led K. Budde, in 1898, to propound the view that we have here in the Canticles the text-book of the Judean wedding. It might have seemed at first sight a difficult task to mould the poem to such an interpretation, but as not only Budde himself but Siegfried have made it the basis of their Commentaries, and as the results of their labours have been accepted by T. K. Cheyne, Cornill and other eminent men, it merits the most careful consideration. One thing is quite certain—to make such exegesis possible, considerable portions of the poem must be struck out as glosses. This subject has been gone into elsewhere[1], and it is enough to say here that in our opinion these emendations, made to support an exegetical theory, are inadmissible, and in considering the theory we shall generally abide by the text as it stands.

(a) It is an enormous assumption that these wedding ceremonies described by Wetzstein as taking place in Syrian villages near Damascus in 1861 were necessarily the same in weddings in Judea more than 2000 years earlier, or at any time. What is often said of "the unchanging East" is quite sound, and these peculiar institutions may be ancient in Syria, but there are many reasons to render even this rather doubtful. In this long space of time, Syria has been under many governments—Greek, Sassanian, Roman, Saracen, Turkish; it has

[1] Excursus II., *post.*

been in religion Persian, Christian, Moslem; and, more than all, it has changed its language. It can hardly be doubted that the complete victory of the Arab language must have been accompanied by the introduction of Arab culture and habits of life. The *wasfs* or songs of which Wetzstein gives specimens are thoroughly Arabic, and there is no proof that such songs were ever composed in Aramean. But, if every detail of the ceremonies of 1861 was going on north of Damascus *cir.* B.C. 250, there is certainly no proof that the marriage on the threshing-floor, the use of the threshing sledge as a throne, the sword dance, the *wasf*, the designation of the married pair as *king* and *queen*, and the other details above referred to, were a regular part of a Judean wedding. There is no evidence to that effect, all the extant evidence is the other way.

Weddings are referred to in Gen. xxix. 22; Judg. xiv. 10; Esther ii. 18; Tob. viii. 19, xi. 19; and the one characteristic and essential feature of all these instances is the seven (or even fourteen) days מִשְׁתֶּה, which seems to have been a feast or banquet daily renewed. The same feature is prominent in the Jewish weddings described in the New Testament, whether in *fact*, John ii., or in *parable*, Matt. xxii. 1—14, xxv. 10. So much was this the case that the LXX. in Gen. xxix. 22 uses γάμον as the equivalent of מִשְׁתֶּה, and in the New Testament ποιεῖν γάμον or γάμους means "to give the marriage feast." The notions of "marriage" and "banquet" seem to have become interchangeable. Now it is singular that in all these accounts there is not a word to suggest that any of the Syrian practices above referred to formed part of the proceedings, and indeed the accounts in John ii. and Matt. xxii. are absolutely inconsistent with any such idea. We know from these accounts what a Jewish wedding feast was like about A.D. 30—was it any different *cir.* B.C. 250? which is the date (according to Budde and Siegfried) when the Song was written. The account in John ii. regards the cheerful and hospitable use of wine as the note of the marriage feast, and it agrees with this that the LXX. use πότον as the equivalent of מִשְׁתֶּה in Judg. xiv. 10 and Esther ii. 18.

(*b*) All general arguments, then, are against the idea of regarding this Israelite poem as embodying the Syrian marriage customs described by Wetzstein. If it is to be proved, it must be proved out of the poem itself, and this can only be done by an extraordinary method of allegorizing, by which everything means something different from what it says. Let us first look for the *threshing-wain*; it is said to be present in a most unlikely place, Cant. iii. 6—11.

In this passage a watcher in Jerusalem sees a procession coming out of the open country and approaching the city, preceded by clouds of dust with which, as it approaches nearer, precious odours are perceived to be intermingled. From the dust emerges a stately litter or palanquin of cedar wood with silver pillars, gilded back, purple seat and other adornments. Seated in the litter is King Solomon, wearing a crown of precious materials, one bearing reminiscences of some joyous incident in his life. Beside it march a bodyguard of sixty *Gibborim*, the well-known name given to David's *corps d'élite*, well armed and ready to beat off a night attack. The procession passes through the streets and disappears from view.

There is no lady in the procession at all. Solomon sits in the litter alone.

This is what the poet described. Siegfried will now tell us what he meant.

"The indispensable harvest tackle of the Syrian peasant, which is often all the furniture he has, the threshing-wain, plays a very special *rôle* in weddings. It serves the bridegroom and the bride as a seat of honour (*merteba*) set up on a high platform after the bridesmaids have first adorned it with embroidered cushions, iii. 10. There they sit, as it were, on their *throne*, honoured during the wedding week as *king and queen*. The wedding week according to this custom is called the *king's week* as well, and fills up the seven days of the wedding. The bridegroom or young husband, although in reality only a poor peasant or shepherd, i. 7, 8; vi. 3, yet passes during the wedding week as king, i. 4, 12; vii. 6, and is celebrated as such in the wedding songs which are sung to him. It is therefore natural that the poets in their descriptions catch at the image of the finest and most brilliant royal figure which Israelite history knows. The bridegroom in his wedding crown is compared with the diadem-bedecked Solomon, the miserable threshing-wain on which he sits becomes Solomon's expensive

litter, the young shepherds who accompany him as רֵעִים or
דוֹדִים v. 1*b*, or as חברים i. 7; viii. 13...into the bridal chamber
become the sword-armed lifeguards of the mighty king..."
p. 87.

Could the poet really have meant all this? Let us look
first at some obvious differences of representation. The procession moves and passes away. The threshing-wain remains
on its platform for a week. Solomon is adorned with a
precious crown. The Syrian bridegroom is not crowned[1].
But, worst of all, in a description of a wedding feast lasting
seven days, the bride or queen is not mentioned at all, although she is sitting there all the time. We cannot believe
that when the poet wrote "King Solomon" he meant "a
peasant," when he described the "litter" he meant "a threshing-wain on a platform," that when he wrote "coming up from
the desert" he meant "standing still," that when he wrote
"*gibborim*" he meant "groomsmen," that when he wrote
"crowned" he did not mean "crowned," and that when he
omitted to name the bride he meant to imply that she was the
centre of the whole affair. What he really says is intelligible.
What he is made to mean is—to use a word of Siegfried's
own—*hokus-pokus*[2].

The *queen* is not mentioned in the poem at all. Again we
turn to Siegfried: "They sought out in her praise as a comparison the handsomest woman who ever in Israel's history
adorned a royal *harem*. She is in vii. 1 called הַשּׁוּלַמִּית, which
often treated by the editors as a proper name[3] has led to the
standing designation Sulammit for the bride of Cant.: it is,
however, as appears from the article, a place-name, and means
'the Sulamite.' With a slight change of liquids we have here
the same name as הַשּׁוּנַמִּית, wherewith in 1 Kings i. 3, 15;
ii. 17, 21 f. Abisag of Sunem (now Solam) is named, of whose
beauty 1 Kings i. 3 f. tells. In reality a poor shepherdess or
vintager, browned by hard work in the vineyards under the
sun, i. 7, and occupied in the garden, vi. 11; vii. 13; viii. 13,

---

[1] Wetz. in Del. p. 166.

[2] "Eine Sache die durch solchen *Hokuspokus* gestützt werden muss, bricht
von selbst zusammen," p. 83.

[3] This is an error. We know of no editor who ever treated this designation
as a proper name.

the bride is sung of as a model of beauty, a second Abisag"
(88). So, because he ought to have, and has not, mentioned
the queen, he must be held to have done so by comparing the
bride with someone who was *not a queen*.

How can this be so? The poet knows no queens except
those in Solomon's *harem*, vi. 8, nor anything about Syrian
brides. The heroine of his story comes from Shulem or Solem,
and when he wants to name her he calls her "the Shulamite"
without reference to Abisag or anybody else.

We will proceed a little with the *king* and the *queen*. In
vi. 8—9 the poet represents someone, probably Solomon, as
declaring that 60 queens, 80 concubines, and innumerable girls
—obviously his whole harem—have seen and praised the *one*
perfect girl to whom he speaks. How is this to be fitted to the
Syrian wedding theory? First an alteration of the text is
made so as to change the speaker[1]. Then Siegfried explains,
"To the poor peasant who will have hard work to maintain one
wife, and later a family, is assigned suitably to his rôle of *king*
a brilliant Harem such as Solomon had, vi. 8. We need not
think of the young wife as distressed by such a suggestion.
She would certainly rejoice if her new consort's fortune per-
mitted such an arrangement." Budde remarks, "The simple
view that Solomon's Harem had seen the praised one is for the
dramatic view of the book as easy and welcome, as it is bold
for the view represented here, yet it hardly goes beyond what
was possible in the Life's-Drama as represented by the Wedding
festivity."

The fact is that the passage in the poem cannot in either of
these ways be made applicable to a village wedding.

In i. 17 the poet describes a delightful spot in a woodland
glade:

> "our couch is green.
> The beams of our houses are cedars,
> And our rafters cypresses."

On this Budde observes: "This is more suitable to the idea
of the distant country lover as the opposite of King Solomon
than to a wedding," so he alters the text[2]. Siegfried proceeds

---

[1] לִשְׁלֹמֹה for הַמָּה. Budde, p. 32; Siegfried, p. 117.

[2] תִּעֲנֶה for רַעֲנָה.

with his allegory: "The miserable cottage in which she lives
becomes in the Song a Cedar palace, i. 17, her girl friends
become during the *king's week* the daughters of Jerusalem who
belong to the Court retinue of the second Abisag, i. 5; ii. 7;
v. 8, 16; viii. 4 f.[1]; in vi. 8 they are the 60 queens, the 80 concubines, and numberless girls of Solomon's Harem."

Can anyone really feel convinced that all this make-believe
took place at rustic weddings or that our poet really meant
anything of the kind?

We now come to the *sahka*, or sword-dance, danced by the
bride on the wedding day evening, with naked feet, flashing
about a sword, waving a handkerchief in her left hand, by the
light of a fire, and surrounded by a ring of men and women
who stand upright while the *wasf* is sung by a solo singer who
is accompanied by the chorus, who sing the refrain with light
movements of their bodies and a gentle clapping of hands[2].
This dance is of Bedouin origin, and may therefore not have
existed in Syria before the Arab period, but we will assume
that it did. Now what is the proof offered that such a dance
formed an essential part of Jewish weddings? It is found in
the phrase כִּמְחֹלַת הַמַּחֲנָיִם. The meaning of this word *Mahanaim*
is disputed. It has been considered doubtful whether it refers
to the celebrated town east of the Jordan, as the name of that
town never has the article elsewhere[3]. Siegfried and Budde
point it as a plural םֹ?—as in Num. xiii. 19; Deut. xxiii. 15;
Jos. x. 5, xi. 4—and Siegfried translates: *Einen Kriegerischen
Reigentanz, A military dance*; or *der Reigen der Heerlager, The
dance of a military camp*. But the word does not necessarily
mean a *military* camp at all. It is a neutral word "camp." It
is used of the camps of the Israelites in the desert; of Jacob's
funeral cortège, Gen. l. 9; of tent-dwellers in Canaan, Num.
xiii. 19; of Jacob's camps of men and animals, Gen. xxxii. 9; as
well as of military camps. But if the phrase does mean *the dance
of a military camp*, it certainly does not and cannot mean *the*

---

[1] Even better is the following, "Die Gefährtinnen werden so angeredet
weil *infolge der Fiction*, nach der Bräutigam und Braut als König und Königin
behandelt werden, die Scene nach Jerusalem verlegt ist und die Brautjungfern
als Jerusalemmiterinnen bezeichnet sind." Sieg. 95.

[2] Wetz. in Del. 166.

[3] This point is discussed in our note on the translation of vii. 1, *post*.

dance of a bride on her wedding day evening in front of a fire brandishing a sword, for not one of those traits is hinted at, however obscurely, by the poet, except the word *dance*. His phrase would hardly describe the sword-dance if it were securely proved from other sources to be a Jewish institution. How much less can the phrase prove this fact! What proof there is goes the other way. The passage vi. 10—vii. 8 is said to be the *wasf* or song of the sword-dance, and in vii. 2 the *shoes* of the dancer are thought to be praised. But the sword-dance was danced with *naked feet*.

It is impossible to make this passage prove that the sword-dance was practised at village weddings in Judea.

So far it must be evident that the words of our poem cannot establish that the picturesque customs which Wetzstein witnessed in some Syrian villages in 1861 were ever a part of Jewish life. It is equally obvious that they can only be found in the poem by (*a*) assuming their existence, (*b*) allegorising some words of the poem till you find them there. It is only by such a process that the threshing-floor and the threshing-wain and the sword-dance and the bridegroom-peasant-king can be even suggested to be there. Even then one element which ought to be there is not—the queen : one thing is there which ought not to be there—the bridegroom's crown. This theory is not scientifically based, it does not naturally spring from the phenomena. Assume the existence of the customs and the writer will undertake to find them all in the 45th Psalm and to adapt the whole Psalm to a village wedding. It would be much easier to handle than the Canticles.

We come now to the *wasfs* or descriptions of the personal beauties of the man and the woman which appear to be that part of the Syrian customs which Wetzstein expressly compared with Canticles[1]. As he truly says they are far the least interesting portions of the poem. One is practically given twice over (iv. 1—6; vi. 4—8), and they are far less instinct with poetic feeling than the more dramatic movements of the poem. They

---

[1] "Auch in der kleinen unter dem Namen des Hohenliedes in den alt-testamentlichen Kanon aufgenommenen Sammlung von reizenden Hochzeitsliedern und Fragmenten solcher steht der *wasf* (c. 4 to c. 7) an poetischem Werte sehr dem Übrigen nach." Budde, p. xviii.

may well have been existing models (*Schablone*, Wetz.) taken up into his works by the poet. But this by no means proves that they were wedding poems, for descriptions of personal beauty are the very commonplaces of lyric poetry in every land and every age. As they stand in the texture of the poem they are in perfect order. Those put in the mouth of Solomon are fulsome praises of the girl he wishes to win, uttered by a not inexperienced king, who may be thought by the poet to have often used them before, especially as he uses one of them twice. The one uttered by the girl is in answer to a question, v. 9. They all have their suitable place in the development of the story, and although they have some sort of resemblance to a Syrian *wasf*, they do nothing to prove that Syrian customs were in use at Judean weddings, or that the Song describes such a wedding.

Having demonstrated that those parts of the Song which are supposed to prove that Wetzstein's Syrian customs were in use at peasants' weddings in Judea, *cir.* B.C. 250, cannot prove any such thing, it now remains to examine some portions of the poem which are irreconcilable with or opposed to such a theory.

i. 5. Budde has pointed out that this is the only place where the sunburnt country beauty is compared with the town girls with their carefully-preserved complexions, and that no place gives stronger support to the "dramatic" view[1]. It is impossible that any poet could introduce this trait at a rustic wedding where the bridesmaids would be as sunburnt as the bride and accustomed like her to work in fields or vineyards.

i. 7, 8. This little question and answer are equally unsuitable. The girl in distress wants to know where her lover is and receives an unkind scornful answer. There is no need to prove that these verses are unsuitable to the rustic wedding, for Siegfried *strikes them out* as a gloss while Budde suggests a corrupt text.

ii. 15. This is a most delicate touch. A girl shut up in a

---

[1] " Denn dies ist die einzige Stelle wo die ländliche Schöne den Stadtmädchen gegenübergestellt ist, die in ihren vier Wänden und durch sorgsame Verschleierung ihre weisse Haut haben schützen können. Wie keine andere kann unsere Stelle zu einer dramatischen Auffassung des Buches reizen, denn hier wäre wirklich der Keim zu einer Verwicklung gegeben."

house realises that her lover is outside. He cannot see her and begs her to let him hear her voice that he may know that she is there. She does not wish to say anything which the Court-ladies may understand, so she sings a little song which he has heard before, about the *foxes in the vineyard*, by which he will understand that she is surrounded by enemies.

This has nothing to do with any wedding idea, so Siegfried *strikes it out*, and Budde treats it as a separate song, uncon-nected with the context.

iii. 1—5. After the girl has heard the voice of the lover follows very appropriately this *first dream*, in which she seeks him in the town, finds him and brings him to the house of her mother (like a brother, viii. 1, 2). This is finely conceived and appropriate to the action, but has no bearing on a village wedding. So Siegfried explains it as a song sung at the wedding describing an imaginary episode in the life of the married pair. To do this both he and Budde *strike out* the last half of *v.* 4, because a young bride when she had found her husband would take him to their own home. Again Budde suggests a corrupted text[1]. How tasteless all this is!

iv. 8. It is impossible for Siegfried and Budde to make anything of this passage, so they both *strike it out*. And yet in the ordinary interpretation it presents no difficulty. The lover calls to the girl to leave the castle in which she is confined, and the people who surround her, under the figurative phrase of "mountain heights inhabited by wild beasts." But in no way can it be fitted to a village wedding. Cornill also *strikes out* this verse.

v. 2—7. The second dream, so different from the first in its sombre tone and its unhappy conclusion, is treated by Budde and Siegfried as a tale told at the wedding to introduce the *wasf* or description of the physical perfections of the bride-groom, v. 10—16. If so it is entirely pointless, whereas if it

---

[1] "Es handelt sich nicht um eine bei der Mutter wohnende Braut sondern um eine junge Frau die den Mann doch wohl ins eigne Haus geführt haben würde." Sieg.

"Nur als Bruder könnte sie den Geliebten in ihrer Mutter Haus bringen und das findet hier keine Anknüpfung. Auch leidet der Vollbesitz der Gegenwart keine Steigerung noch Zielsetzung mehr. Aber die Sätze werden zum Ersatz für anderes Verlorenes oder Beseitigtes hieher gesetzt sein." Budde.

is treated as part of the story it is significant in every way. For the purpose suggested, any other tale would do equally well.

These instances are enough to shew that the village wedding theory cannot be accommodated to the text of the poem as it stands. To make it possible to maintain this theory, those passages which will not suit must be *struck out*.

The great objection to this theory, however, has yet to be stated, viz. *that it does violence to the structure of the poem as leading up to its grand ethical climax*, viii. 6, 7.

The four adjurations to the daughters of Jerusalem are each placed at the end of a section or episode of the poem marking a definite pause in its action, and three of them, ii. 7, iii. 5, and viii. 4, most certainly reflect upon and point the moral of the section which they close, while the fourth, v. 8, contains elements common to ii. 7 and viii. 4, namely sickness caused by love, and a longing for the absent beloved. The moral is the very striking one : *Do not wake, do not excite love until it pleases (love to wake)*. It must be part of the deliberate design of the author to enunciate this sentiment at suitable pauses of his work. It is his *leit-motif* which he wishes from time to time to impress on the reader, and it is the underlying structure of the poem. At every crisis, sad or joyful, he says in effect, *Remember this, reader, Love must not be forced*.

Now, to begin with, Budde, Siegfried and Cornill all break down the structure.

Budde *strikes out* iii. 5; viii. 4.

Siegfried and Cornill *strike out* viii. 4.

And again it is impossible to see how the sentiment so clearly indicated and so enforced by the author can have any place in poems written to be sung at a wedding. It has no force and no meaning, unless it is connected with some story or transaction where efforts are being made to force unwilling love by gifts, i. 9, or flatteries or pressure. When the real action of the piece is over and love has triumphed, the author utters his sentiment for the last time, viii. 4, in the words of ii. 7, in order that he may lead up to his moral on which his eye has been directed all the time and which is by far the finest poetry in the whole piece.

Love is mighty as death,
Ardent love as strong as Sheol.
Its sparks are sparks of fire,
Its fireflames, fireflames from Yah.
Many waters cannot quench love.
Torrents cannot sweep it away.
If a man should give all the wealth of his house for love,
Men would surely despise him.

If this is to have any point or any ethical value it will not be as a disconnected fragment of a song sung among tasteless *wasfs* at a peasant's wedding feast. It will be the moral of a moving story of love tried and faithful which went through fire and water, and readers will despise the man who tried in vain to buy love, because they have followed the history of the attempt. It is hard to accept any theory of the interpretation of this poem which must at once destroy its structure and make its moral meaningless. Perhaps no explanation hitherto given has disposed of every difficulty in this poem. Perhaps no explanation ever will. But this explanation raises so many difficulties. It requires the reader to introduce into ancient Jewish life in every detail the peculiar customs of obscure Syrian tribes observed in 1861, it allegorises in an extraordinary fashion some portions of the poem and cuts out others which are in its way, it takes away all the moral and ethical value of the poem, and when all is done it makes it thoroughly uninteresting.

Finally, what on this theory can be made of the title?

How could the collector of these 23 songs, some only mutilated fragments, sung at weddings, call his formless mosaic "the finest of all poems" and state that Solomon was the author? He must have known, far better than any critic can know now, the quality of the material he had collected[1], and could not think that what he had put together was one poem, when he had just made it out of several[2]. It is not to be believed, except on a hypothesis of deliberate mystification, that such a title could have been affixed to the poem if the poem had been what this theory would make it.

[1] "How comes it that the scribes did not recognize this song which was sung at every Palestinian wedding, and that the playing at being king was so grossly misunderstood?" v. Orelli (Schaff-Herzog, *Enc.*).

[2] "Später *vom Sammler* hinzugefügte Überschrift." Siegfried.

We are convinced that this theory will not endure, although it has gained the suffrages of eminent men. An attempt has been made above to shew with what difficulties it has to contend—and it only remains to say that in view of the phenomena which point so strongly to the *unity* of the poem[1], it is not likely that any *fragmentary* hypothesis will hold the field in the future any more than it has done in the past. Any scheme of interpretation to be successful must interpret the poem *as a whole*.

10. THE PARTS OF THE POEM.

It is now necessary to develop the action of the poem by examining its several parts. In doing so we shall avoid any division into Acts and Scenes or any other indication which would suggest an acting drama. The poet has in the clearest way divided his work into five Cantos, and each of these contains one or more pictures or situations produced by the use of monologue or dialogue. Each of these pictures must be analysed and the effect intended to be produced drawn out of the speeches. Each Canto according to Ewald[2] contains the events of one day—and this seems to be correct—only the days need not be regarded as strictly consecutive, *e.g.* there must be some interval of time between the fourth and fifth. In any event the action of the poem must include a very short space of time, the stress of the emotion is throughout at its height, and the early spring after the winter rains is no further advanced at the end than at the beginning, ii. 13, 15; vi. 11; vii. 13.

CANTO I.

(*a*) i. 2—8. The Shulamite has been brought into the apartments of the palace as she tells us, i. 4, and is surrounded by ladies of the Court whom she, a daughter of Galilee, calls "daughters of Jerusalem," i. 5. This scene is supposed to take place at Jerusalem, and the girl has only just arrived there, and is regarded with some curiosity by the ladies who surround her. They know, and she knows, why she has been brought there, and by whom. While she stands there, sad

---

[1] See Section 4, *sup.*   [2] *Dichter* II. 346.

and solitary, the ladies break forth into a song in praise of Solomon; one voice begins in the name of all, *vv.* 2, 3, and in the exultation of the song passes into the second person[1]. The singer longs for the endearments of the king, which are better than wine, his fame is more widely diffused than the odour of costly unguents, and he is loved by all maidens[2]! This song is designed to impress upon the new-comer the glory and delight of being loved by Solomon, but it has quite a different effect; she thinks of her absent lover, hoping perhaps he may have followed her to Jerusalem, and that perhaps he may be near and may hear her. She utters a cry, whether he can hear or not, that he will help her to escape from these rooms where the king has brought her, *v.* 4 *a*[3]. The pæan of praise is for a moment interrupted by this cry of distress so different in its tone, but when it is uttered the song breaks out again in full chorus; again they declare the king's endearments better than wine—the maidens are right to love him, he is really as charming as they declare him to be, 4 *b*. If this song was intended to impress the Shulamite, it has failed of its object; instead of inclining her towards Solomon it has produced a despairing call to someone else. The Court ladies look in some astonishment at the country beauty, and, confused by this scrutiny, she expresses the hope that though she is *black*, like the tents of the Bedouin[4], woven of goats' hair, she may yet be *comely*, as the royal pavilions which recently made a sojourn near her country home. Her dark complexion may indeed make a startling contrast with the fair complexions of these town ladies, but she is sun-burnt. Angry brothers have sent her into the vineyard there to be glared upon by the scorching sun, but ah! her own vineyard, all that is her own, her beauty, her liberty, herself, she has not kept, *vv.* 5, 6. Relieved for a time from

---

[1] Such enallage is not uncommon in Heb. poetry. See Deut. xxxii. 15; Is. i. 29, v. 8; Jer. xxix. 19; *Ges. K.* 144. 4 p.

[2] עֲלָמוֹת. The same word as vi. 8—harem-ladies.

[3] It should be noticed by what delicate gradations the poet brings the lovers together. In i. 4 she neither sees nor hears her betrothed; in ii. 8 she sees and hears him, he hears but does not see her; in iv. 8 they see and hear each other; in vii. 12 and viii. 5 they are together.

[4] *Kedar* is used as a general name for the nomads of N. Arabia. Is. xxii. 16 (with Cheyne's note), lx. 7; Ps. cxx. 5.

this scrutiny her thoughts turn again to him whom her soul loves, away in Galilee, as he wanders freely about the open country with his flock, while she is shut up here. Where is he now, where is he making his noontide rest in the heat of the day? Oh that he could tell her himself—for nobody here knows—and she would not wish to wander about among other shepherds and their flocks looking for him. She forgets for a moment that she is not free to wander, v. 7. The Court ladies hear this strange utterance and are astonished. "What? will this beautiful girl, who has the good fortune to be admired by the king whose praise we have just sung, languish for the love of a simple shepherd?" They address to her a scornful answer to her longing question: if she is so foolish as to prefer the shepherd she had better go and follow his tracks, and drive about a herd of goats among shepherds' tents. Such is the life of those who prefer shepherds to kings, and country surroundings to the pomp and luxury in which she may live if she will, v. 8.

Note. Some expositors (Ewald, Ginsburg) would give the whole passage 2—4 to Shul. but not very suitably. She would hardly speak of her country lover as surrounded by the perfume of precious unguents, or as one whose fame is widespread, still less as one whom the harem-ladies love. These traits belong to Solomon, and indicate him as the subject of the song. Oettli gives *v.* 8 to "the friend." But as has already been shewn[1] the phrase, "Oh fairest among women," is characteristic of the "daughters of Jerusalem" and must be spoken by them.

(b) i. 9—ii. 7. Solomon is now present and, struck by the beauty and noble bearing of the Shulamite, begins to address her with compliments. He compares her to a favourite mare which he was accustomed to drive in the chariots he had received from the Egyptian Pharaoh, no doubt a more flattering comparison than it might appear to modern taste[2], v. 9. Her fine cheeks and neck were adorned with simple ornaments, these should be replaced by costlier ones of gold and silver, more suited to the gorgeous life of the Court, vv. 10, 11. Now follows a singularly curious though perfectly natural dialogue.

[1] Section 6, *sup.*

[2] For Solomon's importations of horses, mares and chariots from Egypt see 1 Kings v. 6, x. 26 (LXX.), 29 ; 2 Chron. i. 17. For parallels to the comparison from Horace and Theokritus, see Del. and Gins. *Comms. ad loc.*

Not a word does the Shulamite say in direct reply to any speech which Solomon may address to her. Every speech she utters refers to and expresses her attachment to the absent one (*v.* 7), the "beloved." Of Solomon's compliments and promises she does not take the least notice. While the king was away the thought of the beloved one surrounded her with an atmosphere of perfume. It was as though she carried in her bosom a bag or bottle of fragrant nard[1] or myrrh, or a cluster of sweet flowers of henna. His image was always with her wherever she went, even in this palace, and the presence of the king was an unwelcome interruption of this delightful memory, *vv.* 12, 13, 14.

Solomon understands perfectly well that these praises are not intended for him; it is not likely that a country girl would address him as "my beloved," her thoughts are somewhere else, but he does not choose to notice it. So he resumes his compliments—*her eyes are doves, v.* 15, charming in colour, graceful in movement[2]. She hears this flattery but instead of responding to it, she addresses the reply to the absent beloved. *Am I fair? Thou art fair my beloved, and pleasant,* and, regardless of the presence of the king, her thoughts fly away to happy days when she roamed with her lover in woodland glades, sitting on a divan of green moss, with overarching cedars and cypresses forming a majestic roof; how different a scene from this palace where she is now confined. This is no place for a simple country girl. I am only a *narcissus* on the plain of Sharon[3], a *lily* growing in the valley, a modest country flower not fit for Courts, ii. 1. Once again the king tries a compliment, ingeniously combining it with her last phrase and declaring that, country girl as she is, she stands out among the beauties of the Court like *a lily among thorns.* It is of no

---

[1] Such smelling bags or bottles (בָּתֵּי הַנֶּפֶשׁ) are mentioned among the ornaments of Jewish ladies, Is. iii. 20. They were probably hung round the neck by a thread.

[2] See Ps. lxviii. 14.

[3] This is not the well-known plain of Sharon between Joppa and Caesarea, but the one in Galilee mentioned in the *Onomasticon*, "Usque in presentem diem regio inter montem Thabor et stagnum Tiberiadis *Saronas* adpellatur," which was therefore close to her home at Shulem. See Del. and Budde's *Comm. ad loc.*; Lagarde, *Onomastica Sacra*, ed. alt. pp. 185, 286.

avail, her heart is fixed on another, and taking the colour of her speech from the king's, she declares that her beloved is *like an apple tree* among wild trees, dispensing fragrance and sweetness, *fruit* and *shade*. At this point Solomon disappears from the picture. We do not know whether he is present or not, as the maid recalls past scenes of happiness; how she and her lover rambled about the vine-clad hills, and his affection seemed to overshadow her like a banner, *vv.* 3, 4. At this point the pressure of conflicting emotions grows too great to be borne. The feeling of captivity, the words of the ladies, the compliments of the king, the memory of past delights, the thoughts of the beloved, all press on her. She is ready to faint, she calls for some refreshment, *for I am sick with love, v.* 5. She utters a longing cry for the strong arm which could best support her, *v.* 6, and summons all her strength to adjure the Court ladies to cease their efforts to awaken in her an affection for Solomon. She adjures them by the animals that are lovely and free, which roam about the open country. So free and unconfined, so natural and delightful should love be. *Stir not up and awaken not love until love pleases to awake.*

Note. v. 15 is ascribed by Oettli to "the friend." But the expression "my friend" is characteristic of Solomon, to whom the speech is given above[1].

CANTO II.

(*a*) ii. 8—17. The Shulamite describes, in impassioned monologue, an interview with her beloved. He has followed her from Galilee, has arrived at Jerusalem, found out where the ladies of Solomon's harem live, and is resolved to speak with her if he can. She hears a sound, she feels that he is there, and immediately she imagines the light and rapid steps with which he has crossed the mountains between her country home and the city. *See, there he is,* standing behind the courtyard wall, trying to gaze through one latticed window after another in vain. He cannot see her, he does not know where to look, he dare not ask for admittance, and she dare not say that she has seen him, *v.* 8. But, in hopes that somehow she may hear him, he utters a cry. Is it possible that she may be able to

---

[1] Section 6, *sup.*

escape from this captivity ? He cannot tell, but he will ask her.
So he begins, *Up, my friend, my fair one, and come away.* He
describes the beauties of opening spring *in our land,* our country
home. The latter rain is over and the whole country side has
burst into bloom. *The flowers appear* (reminding her of the
narcissus and the lily to which she likened herself, ii. 1). Men
and birds alike are singing with the joy of spring. Figs are
ripening, the grapes in the vineyard are blossoming. *Up, my
friend, my fair one, and come away.* It is no time to be shut up
within walls in a town, come and enjoy the beauty of spring in
our country home, *vv.* 11, 12, 13! Then he suddenly realises that
she is a prisoner and his tone changes, for he feels that she is
inaccessible to him. So he addresses her in a bold figure as
a dove, dwelling in the clefts of a high rocky steep to which he
cannot climb, a precipice where she is so hidden away that he
cannot even see her[1]. Oh that she would shew her face, but
if that is impossible, as he cannot see through the latticed
windows, *let me hear thy voice, for sweet is thy voice, v.* 14. In
response to this call she sings a snatch of a vineyard song
which, though well known to him, will convey no meaning to
any of the ladies who surround her in the palace. This little
song is well chosen, it is an allegory of her situation. Just as
the little foxes are *destroyers of vineyards*[2], so she is in peril
from these ladies who surround her and would destroy *her own
vineyard* (i. 5), her personal honour and self-respect, *v.* 15. She
perceives that he has heard her, and she ventures in guarded
language to assure him of her unchanged affection. She is not
Solomon's but *his,* the shepherd's, *v.* 16. Then feeling the peril to
which he exposes himself by lingering about in the neighbourhood of the harem, and having assured him of her fidelity, she
bids him to flee away *like a gazelle on the mountains,* and not to
return to so dangerous a situation until the evening breeze
brings safe and sheltering darkness, *v.* 17[3].

[1] The wood pigeon builds its nest in clefts of the rocks (see Obad. 3 ;
Jer. xlix. 16) and other steep rocky ravines; comp. Jer. xlviii. 28, "Become like
the dove who builds her nest beyond the yawning abyss."

[2] The foxes destroy or injure the vineyards, because by driving holes and
passages in the ground, they bore through the soil and loosen it (Neh. iii. 35) so
that the growth and prosperity of the vines suffer injury. Hitzig, *Comm.*

[3] יָפ֫וּחַ, *breathes forth.* The allusion is to the cool breeze arising in the
evening to temper the heat of the day. See Gen. iii. 8, xxiv. 63 ; also Is. xxi. 4,

Note. Most interpreters of this passage have viewed it either as a scene of her earlier life related by Shul. or as a vision called up by her excited fancy. It seems however much simpler to conclude that the poet meant to picture a real occurrence. In the structure of his poem, a meeting of Shul. and her lover is followed by an agitated dream ending a Canto. ii. 8—17 interview, iii. 1—5 dream

iv. 8—v. 1 „ v. 2—8 „

and this cannot be accidental. The theory that Shul. relates an incident of the past is probably the result of the scheme of dramatic representation and the difficulty of staging the scene. No such difficulty arises in the interpretation of a dramatic poem[1], where the poet simply puts his picture in the mouth of Shul. And there are many traits in the picture very unsuited to a visit of the lover to Shul. in her home. Would it be natural for him to recount the beauties of the opening spring *in our land* to a country maiden who had seen them all the day before and could see them then by looking out of the window, or to tell the vineyard-guardian that the vines were in bloom (see vi. 12)? Could a girl living in her mother's house be suitably described as a dove hidden in unaccessible precipices? There is distress and emotion in the call in *v.* 14, and a sense of danger. It is something more than the wish of a happy lover to see the face of his adored one and hear her sing. And if interpreted as an actual occurrence the scene takes an appropriate and suitable place in the progress and development of the story, whereas if regarded either as an episode of the past or as a vision of a heated fancy, it is of no value and leads to nothing.

(*b*) iii. 1—5. The Shulamite relates to the Court ladies a dream she had in the night following the interview with the beloved described ii. 8—17. This dream flows naturally from what has preceded it, the longing for her lover, i. 7, 8, her captivity in a town (*v.* 2), and her knowledge that her lover has also been in the town, and the art of the poet has imparted to it the vague atmosphere of uncertainty and the inconsequence of action which belong to a dream. In vision she seeks her lover in the house where she is, and cannot find him. She wanders through the streets and open places of the great unknown city looking for him. It is night and she finds no-one but the night watchmen on their rounds[2]. She asks them, with that utter disregard of probabilities which occurs in

"the twilight that I love." "The shadows flee away when they become longer and longer, when they stretch out (Ps. cix. 23, cii. 12) and gradually disappear." Del.

[1] Section 5, *sup.*

[2] Ps. cxxvii. 1; Is. xxi. 11, lxii. 6.

dreams, whether they have seen someone whom she does not name, and whom they cannot know, and she does not wait for an answer. At last she finds him, she holds him, and the scene changes. She is in Shulem, and is bringing him to her mother's house. It is the same feeling which she expresses again, viii. 1, 2. If she could meet him outside this palace, she would bring him to her mother's house, the suitable place for the betrothed to be with her lover. Her sentiments are always the same, waking or sleeping, whether he is present or absent, and whatever the king may urge. *My beloved is mine and I am his.* So at the end of this Canto she again adjures the Court ladies to make no further effort to awaken in her an affection for Solomon. I have seen my beloved in the city. I dream of him in the night. He fills my thoughts, there is no room for any other. *Stir not up and awaken not love until love pleases to wake*[1].

CANTO III.

(*a*) iii. 6—11. The poet depicts a scene which displays "Solomon in all his glory," not only to shew to the Shulamite but also to his readers or auditors the pomp and majesty of this king, what an honour it is to be loved by him, and what a contrast he offers to the young farmer in Galilee! The whole picture is a comment on the words we have already heard, *Ah! they are in the right who love thee*, i. 4. A procession comes from the open country and approaches the city, preceded by clouds of dust, intermingled with precious odours. From the dust emerges a stately litter or palanquin of cedar adorned with gold, silver, purple and other ornaments. Seated in the litter is King Solomon wearing a precious crown. Around it are sixty veteran body-guards, drawn from David's corps of heroes[2], well armed and ready to beat off a night attack. The

---

[1] It should be observed that there is a *progress* in the attitude of the Court ladies to Shul. In i. 8 they are scornful. Here apparently indifferent. In v. 9 interested. In vi. 1 sympathetic.

[2] These were the famous 600, הַגִּבֹּרִים, David's heroic body-guard, who were with him at Gath (1 Sam. xxvii. 3, xxx. 9), whose leaders were noted for valiant exploits (2 Sam. xxiii.), and who effected Solomon's succession (1 Kings i. 8, 10). They are not afterwards heard of except in this poem, though their barracks are named, Neh. iii. 16.

king has been away from his capital for some royal purpose, and the women of the capital come out of their houses to see the royal procession pass through the streets.

Note. This passage is usually (under the influence of the stage idea) assigned to some watchman or spectator, but from the point of view of a dramatic poem the matter is of no moment.

It has been thought by many writers that this scene represents a marriage procession and that the bride is in the litter. It is difficult to see any foundation for either view in the text. The litter, says the poet, was as regards its interior inlaid with love[1], and whatever this means it points to some sort of decoration. "We cannot speak of being paved or tapestried with persons" (Del.), and it seems quite certain that it is not intended to represent that there is any lady in the procession at all (so Budde, Oettli). And indeed if there were a bride, who could it be? Ewald places *the Shulamite* there. "The unexpected resistance Solomon has encountered has decided him to raise her to the rank of a full queen-consort and to marry her with royal pomp." It is simply impossible to accept this view. It has already been shewn[2] that the latter part of the poem is only intelligible on the assumption that the heroine is not yet married, and that no relation which could be called marriage was possible between Solomon and the Shulamite, nor in the later speeches of the king is there a word to suggest that such a marriage had taken place.

Other editors have suggested other ladies as brides in this supposed marriage train, *e.g.* "one of the daughters of Jerusalem" (Hitzig), "une beauté nouvelle qu'il amène à son sérail" (Renan), or, most surprising of all, "a Tyrian princess" (Bruston). It is difficult to think that the poet could have meant anything of this kind, or to attribute to him such an utter want of taste. Not only is there nothing in the words he has used to lead to any such assumption, but it is utterly foreign to the purpose and meaning of his poem. The problem of the story, its interesting complication, is clear enough. "Will the gifts and flatteries of the king prevail over the Shulamite or will she resist him to the end and remain true to her beloved?"

---

[1] Hitzig alters אַהֲבָה to אֲהֻבָה, "a beloved," but this does not help.

[2] Section 8.

She has seen her lover and made it plain that, waking or sleeping, her thoughts are entirely fixed upon him. So to heighten the temptation and to shew what she has to resist, a picture of regal splendour is introduced. It is not conceivable that any poet should be so entirely devoid not only of good taste but of right feeling as to represent Solomon at this critical juncture, when all trembles in the balance, not only being married to some other woman, but leading her in solemn procession through the streets under the very eyes of the girl he wishes to subjugate. Nothing but the most direct statement could compel belief in a situation so antecedently incredible. And there is another objection to this view which goes even deeper. The poet intends to represent Solomon as really impressed by the beauty and charm of the Shulamite. Among the ladies of his Court she is to him (for the moment) *a lily among thorns*. Like all men of his kind, he is very serious while the fancy lasts. It is not psychologically true, it is not really possible, that during the few days within which the action of this poem is confined, he should be thought of as turning aside to court another woman, and then resuming his pursuit of the Shulamite as if nothing had happened. Even from a versatile lover like Solomon this was not to be expected. No, this procession is not to be thought of as a marriage train.

The view that this passage represents a marriage has really arisen from reminiscences of the old traditional exegesis which regarded this poem as an epithalamium, and which we have already examined in Delitzsch's representation of it[1]. We must repeat that there is no wedding in the piece, the keynote is successful resistance (viii. 10) to the intruder and a joyful anticipation of a future marriage, iv. 16—v. 1, but the marriage itself is outside the frame of this poem.

It has been thought, however, that a marriage train must be implied from the words in *v.* 11.

> "In the crown wherewith his mother crowned him
> On his marriage day
> And on the day of the gladness of his heart."

Now it must be remembered that the word "crown" here does not mean a "wreath" or "chaplet" but a diadem of gold

---

[1] "Epithalamium libellus hic id est nuptiale carmen dramatis in modum mihi videtur a Salamone conscriptus." Origen, de la Rue, III. 26 A.

or other precious materials[1]. It will also be noted that according-
ing to our poem Solomon must be thought of as having at its
date 60 queens and a host of inferior ladies, vi. 8. If then the
" crown " in our passage has anything to do with marriage, this
would lead to the curious conclusion that it was the custom
of the queen-mother to give the king a golden crown on every
marriage day, and that she must therefore have done so at
least 60 times! It is not to be supposed that the poet means or
could possibly mean this. Some special, significant, crown must
be meant, connected with the happy memory of some special
significant day in the king's life, a day which must be at once
"his marriage day" and "the day when his heart rejoiced."

Can such a special day be found in the traditions of
Solomon's life and such as would be well known to the poet?
We think it can.

When Solomon came to the throne he was surrounded with
difficulties. The death of the mighty David was a signal to
the enemies he had subjugated to reassert themselves. These
enemies had in David's lifetime been able to find refuge in
Egypt (2 Sam. viii. 13 f.), and the growing power of this
neighbouring empire under the 21st dynasty was a serious
menace to the young king of Israel. How serious the danger
was we may realise by considering the invasion of Judah under
Sheshonk, in the days of Solomon's son and successor (1 Kings
xiv. 25 f.). From this danger on the side of Egypt Solomon
succeeded in extricating himself by a treaty under which he
married the daughter of the reigning Pharaoh, and, perhaps by
some recognition of Egyptian supremacy in South Palestine,
received as a dowry the important fortress of Gezer, which the
Egyptian king conquered and handed over to him[2]. Such a

---

[1] עֲטָרָה where not used figuratively as Is. xxviii. 1, Job xix. 9, and often in
Prov., is always conjoined with costly materials

　　　　　　2 Sam. xii. 30　זָהָב וְאֶבֶן יְקָרָה,
　　　　　　Esth. viii. 15　זָהָב,
　　　　　　Zech. vi. 11　כֶּסֶף־וְזָהָב,
　　　　　　Ps. xxi. 4　פָּז,

as the insignia of royal or priestly dignity.

"Die Übersetzung Kranz statt Krone ist dicht neben בַּמֶּלֶךְ שְׁלֹמֹה ganz
unmöglich." Budde.

[2] 1 Kings iii. 1, ix. 15. Kittel, Gesch. des V. Isr. ii. 220. Maspero, Hist.
Anc. ii. 738. Ewald, Hist. E. T., iii. 220.

marriage was of the highest importance to the young king. It gained him a powerful ally, a safe southern frontier, and most important trade openings, as well as a young bride. He built for this young queen a special house (1 Kings vii. 8, ix. 24), and among his crowd of later wives she stood out as distinguished from them (1 Kings xi. 1)[1]. Surely it was the day of this marriage beyond all others which stood out pre-eminently as *his marriage day and the day of his heart's joy*. Such a day was worth a golden crown, and we may well conclude that the crown his mother placed on his head on that momentous day became the symbol of his regality.

The poet knew all this, and in giving a picture of the splendour of Solomon he places on the head of the king this royal diadem. It is not *marriage* pomp but *royal* pomp that he desires to emphasise in this scene.

(*b*) iv. 1—7. A speech of Solomon in praise of the Shulamite who apparently listens to it in silence. This praise is entirely confined to physical perfections: nowhere in the poem does the king seem to look for or desire any other charms than those of the body. With some art he is made to draw his comparisons from country life. After repeating one of his former compliments, *thine eyes are doves*, i. 15, he proceeds to compare her black and flowing *tresses* to a flock of black goats flowing, as it were, down a mountain slope in Gilead[2]—her white and regular *teeth* to a flock of sheep shorn and washed, appearing in dazzling whiteness and each with twins, as each of the teeth has its fellow—the *lips* of the firmly closed mouth *like a scarlet thread*, and the *mouth* itself comely (though it will not speak). The *temples*, including the upper part of the cheek, are as finely rounded and as delicately coloured as the outer portion of a pomegranate. Then, with a comparison more suitable to a king, the proud *neck* adorned with a necklace (*v.* 9, also i. 10) is compared to a tower of David[3], an arsenal on which were

---

[1] It is curious that this is the only one of Solomon's marriages to which the author of 1 Kings applies the word חתן. Comp. יִתְחַתֵּן iii. 1 with יְהִי־לוֹ נָשִׁים xi. 3.

[2] Gilead was especially a country of flocks, Num. xxxii. 1; Jer. l. 19; Mic. vii. 14.

[3] Probably "the tower of the flock" on Ophel-Zion, Mic. iv. 8; Neh. iii. 25. That shields were hung on such towers, Ezek. xxvii. 11; 1 Macc. iv. 57.

suspended a thousand shields. Finally returning to country comparisons, the *breasts* shimmering through a light garment are like twin fawns feeding among lilies. There is no reply to this array of compliments—the Shulamite's thoughts are with some-one else. So, as Solomon seems to be unable to obtain any response, he announces that until evening he will withdraw to his odorous garden of exotic plants. The *myrrh* and *frankin-cense* are both literal and figurative, he will return in the twilight with the sweet odours of the garden spices in his garments and fragrant love-longings in his heart. But as he departs he brings out one parting thought, *fair is his friend, and without a blemish.*

(c) iv. 8—v. 1. In this picture the lover appears. Just at the time when the Shulamite is oppressed by the anxious thought that the king, although he has withdrawn for the time, will come again in the evening; and while she looks forward with terror to this visit, a voice, a well-known voice, is heard outside. The beloved speaks in strange metaphorical language, he dare not express himself plainly, for he does not know that his words will reach his betrothed, but others may hear them and it may bring danger to her, or to him, if his words are too clearly understood. So he speaks in a figure, and describes her present situation as though she were on some inaccessible height of Lebanon or Hermon[1], surrounded by savage beasts. But perilous as her position is, dangerous as are the enemies by whom she is surrounded, she shall yet escape. *With me thou shalt journey* from this unhappy place! *v.* 8. The maiden shews herself, wearing a necklace which he recognizes (see i. 10), and the sight of her fills him with courage, *v.* 9. He forgets, or he rises above, the dangers of his position at one glance from her, and breaks out into expressions of admira-tion and affection. But his praise is very different from Solo-mon's. The king never rises higher than the praise of various

---

[1] Lebanon is the whole west side of Coele-Syria. Amana, Senir and Hermon seem to be names of, or to indicate parts of, the great snow-crowned outrunner of the Antilibanus. See Deut. iii. 9. "The Sidonians call Hermon *Sirion* (Ps. xxix. 6) and the Amorites call it *Senir*" (Ezek. xxvii. 5; 1 Chr. v. 23). *Amana* is the Assyrian name of Hermon. See Buhl, *Geog. des alt. Paläst.,* p. 110 fol.; Lagarde, *Onom.* 126, 238. Panthers (*nimr*) are still found in Palestine. See for an adventure with one not far from Shunem, Thomson, *The Land and the Book,* c. 29.

bodily features, he never thinks of virtues or charms of mind and
character. The lover thinks otherwise. He praises indeed her
caresses and her sweet discourses, for in happy days of the
past he has enjoyed them (ii. 3, 4), and he expresses his wonder
at the perfumes with which she has been loaded in the palace[1],
and of which the fragrance is borne to him, *vv.* 10, 11. But he
turns from these thoughts to express his confidence in her
constancy and virtue, even in her present desperate situation,
by a lovely image. He pictures a *locked garden*, secure from
entry by any but the rightful owner, even locked against
himself, she is only his *betrothed sister*. This garden is filled
with the choicest fruits and the sweetest and most fragrant
spice trees, and abundantly watered with the purest and coolest
waters, and the *fountain* is *sealed*, that it may be kept pure.
"The picture is a purely ideal one...the beauties and attractions
of both north and south, of Lebanon with its streams of sparkling water and fresh mountain air, of En-gedi with its tropical
climate and henna plantations, of the spice-groves of Arabia
Felix and of the rarest products of the distant mysterious Ophir
must all combine to furnish out one glorious representation,
'Thou art all fair[2].'" It is the praise of a virtuous maiden
and the expression of perfect trust born of intimate acquaintance, *vv.* 12—15.

To this delightful figure the Shulamite responds by taking
up the metaphor. "Come any experience which may render
my garden more fragrant to my beloved. For is it not to be
his garden? Whether *north wind or south wind* blow, let them
make me pleasing to him. He has called me *Betrothed*. May
the happy time arrive when he may enjoy *the precious fruits* of
the garden he describes so rapturously." She joyfully anticipates the future marriage day, *v.* 16. The beloved is not slow
to reply to this. To his delighted fancy that happy day has
already arrived. He has no doubt of the future—the dangers
and difficulties of the present seem to disappear, already the
locked garden seems to open its portals to him—and with this
joyous certainty the picture is completed, *v.* 1.

Note. It was thought by Ewald that the whole of this passage is
a monologue by the Shulamite, whose excited fancy seemed to hear her

[1] As to the customs of the harem in regard to perfumes, see Esth. ii. 12;
also Ps. xlv. 9.   [2] Kingsbury, p. 688.

friend speaking and repeated his words—words which the beloved had
actually spoken to her on some former occasion. But there seems no
necessity for so violent an assumption. In the former scene, ii. 17, there is
reason given to suppose that he will return—and as is remarked above, in
the structure of the poem, his two appearances precede and naturally lead
up to the Shulamite's two dreams. And it must be felt that the contrast
produced by hearing the voice of the 'beloved' immediately after that of
Solomon is very powerful. Here again it is well to remember that there
is no question of scenic representation, but a series of pictures, and that
the actual presence of the 'beloved' produces a progress in the action of
the piece.

(d) v. 2—8. The Shulamite relates to the Court ladies,
on the morning following this eventful day, a dream which she
has had in the preceding night. Excited by the royal progress, the king's wooing, the lover's visit, her agitated mind
has blended various traits of these events into one confused
dream-picture. The address, v. 2, combines Solomon's phrase
"my friend" with the lover's epithet "my sister," and with
"my dove" of both. The luxury of the palace, "the finest
myrrh," v. 5, is in juxtaposition with the young shepherd wet
with the nightly dew[1], v. 2. This dream resumes many touches of
the former dream—the presence of the lover, the search for him,
the wandering in the streets of the city, the watchmen, and
the general atmosphere of dreamy inconsequence—but the tone
is sombre and, in distinction from the former vision, the issue
is unhappy. In the former dream "*I found him*," in this
"*I found him not.*" The poet has shewn much art in depicting
this changed atmosphere, which demonstrates that the action
of the poem has progressed since the first dream and is rising
to its height.

In vision she seems to have retired to rest when there is
a knocking at the door. The beloved, cold and wet, seeks for
admission. She puts him off with excuses, but relents at once
when she sees his hand put through the hole of the lock to
open it[2]. Then *her heart yearns for him.* She rises and opens
to him but he is gone, he does not answer her call, and her
heart sinks. Then she is wandering in the streets of the city

---

[1] Comp. Gen. xxxi. 40; Judg. vi. 38.

[2] The lock is placed on the inside of the door. To enable the owner to
unlock it a hole is cut in the door through which he thrusts his arm and
inserts the key. See *The Land and the Book*, c. 22, and the plate.

and is maltreated by the watchmen, who take from her the outer garment which, like every Eastern woman, she wears out of doors[1]. So the dream ends, as the maiden stripped, beaten, and unhappy seeks her beloved in vain.

The poem represents her here, as in ii. 7, as unwell as a result of these experiences and emotions. And so the form of the adjuration which closes the Canto is varied here. She does not now feel it needful to urge these ladies who surround her, *not to wake love until it please love to wake.* They have learned, by this time, how it is with her heart. But the beloved may come again and she may be too unwell to see him. So the adjuration this time is, *If you find my beloved, tell him that I am sick with love,* and that if I do not see him, that alone is the reason. The Court ladies have begun, as the next Canto shews, to feel an interest in this 'beloved' who is so strangely preferred to Solomon, and in this girl who has twice been brought by violent emotion into a fainting condition; perhaps even they feel some sympathy for her in the unhappy conflict in which she is involved.

CANTO IV.

(*a*) v. 9—vi. 3. In this picture, the Shulamite, now recovered from her fainting fit, is questioned by the Court ladies as to this "beloved," whom they know she has seen twice and dreamed of twice, to whom she remains so obstinately faithful, and whom, strangely, as it seems, she continues to prefer to Solomon, notwithstanding his regal pomp and all his flatteries. *What is thy beloved more than any other; what is this country-man of thine, whom thou dost prefer to a king?* The Shulamite proceeds to an impassioned description of his manly beauty, first in general terms, v. 10, and then in the detail of the several parts. He is *white and red*[2], the colours which display

---

[1] For this רְדִיד see Is. iii. 23, "a wide shawl for throwing round the shoulders." Del. note.

[2] צַח וְאָדוֹם. Comp. the description of the Jewish nobles, Lam. iv. 7, where the same words are used:

> Her nobles were purer than snow,
> They were *whiter* than milk,
> They were more *ruddy* in body than corals.

the soundest health, and in an army of myriads he would stand out conspicuous as a standard bearer. Then (coming to the various parts); His *head* is beautiful and bright like fine gold. His *locks* are long and waving like palm-branches, and raven-black. *His eyes*, quick glancing on their moist beds, like doves hovering over water brooks, stand out from full well-rounded white orbits. *His cheeks*, charming and round like the beds in a garden (such as she has seen in the palace garden, full of fragrant plants), are covered with manly growths of hair[1]. *His lips* are like red lilies, and distil the myrrh of sweet caresses (see viii. 1). *His fingers* are like golden cylinders, tipped with nails like polished jewels. *His body* is so well-formed that it may be compared to an ivory statue, and the blue robe he wears sets it off like a row of sapphires. *His legs* are firm and well-proportioned like marble columns, and his feet like golden pedestals. Now she returns to the thought of him as a whole, he is *chosen* from among men as the *cedars of Lebanon* are superior in glory and beauty to all the trees of the forest. *His mouth* is all sweetness—and *he himself*, what need to say more—he is *altogether compact of delights*, whatever is most to be desired, that he is. *Such is my beloved*, ye ladies, who ask me what he is, *v.* 16.

The Court ladies become interested. They would like to see this ideal of manly beauty, and as the girl had suggested not long before that they might meet him, *v.* 8, they declare themselves ready to join her in looking for him, vi. 1. But she has no such idea. It would be dangerous to let them know his name or his whereabouts. So she answers in a manner which reveals nothing, except that he is a shepherd. *He has gone down to his garden to feed his flock and gather lilies*, and they may imagine for whom he gathers them. But that these ladies may have no doubt of her continued affection for him she repeats her former words, ii. 16. *He who feeds his flock among the lilies is my beloved. He is mine and I am his.*

(*b*) vi. 4—vii. 1. Solomon once more attempts to win the affection of the Shulamite by flattering speeches, and, as before, never advances beyond praise of her physical beauty. She does not respond but fixes on him a silent look of repulsion and scorn, *v.* 5. His first comparison is worthy of a king.

---

[1] In Numb. vi. 5 the same verb גִּדֵּל is used of letting the hair grow.

She is *as fair as Tirzah*, the beautiful north-country town, *and comely as Jerusalem*[1], but, with those stern looks, as *awe-inspiring as bannered hosts*. He cannot bear her look, it terrifies him, he begs her to turn her eyes away. Confused and discouraged he hardly knows how to go on, and can think of nothing better than repeating his former eulogy of iv. 1—3, a stereotyped flattery which may very well have done service on other occasions, merely soulless compliments, and of which, perhaps through confusion, he leaves out a line. Naturally enough this twice-told tale produces no more effect than it did on the former occasion. So the king turns to another kind of compliment which can hardly fail of its effect. He declares that all the ladies of his Court, not only *queens*, but those of inferior rank, however numerous they may be, are nothing to him in comparison with her who stands before him. She is the *only one* in comparison with all that host, and the *pure one* of her mother, about whom he has no doubt informed himself. But to carry the compliment to its height, he adds that these queens and ladies from the first moment they saw her had united in her praise. He quotes their exclamation of astonishment and praise, *Who is this like the dawn, fair as the white moon, bright as the hot sun*[2], *awe-inspiring as bannered hosts? v.* 10. Surely this praise cannot be without effect: she is not only superior in beauty to the whole of the ladies of the Court, but she herself has heard them admit it. She cannot have forgotten that cry of wonder and admiration, unsought and spontaneous as it was. She has not forgotten it, nor its distressing consequences. The memory of that momentous scene rushes upon her, and without taking any notice of Solomon or his compliments, in a kind of soliloquy or reminiscence she recounts how one day, having gone down to her garden in the *wady* to look for the first signs of opening spring (after the winter rain, ii. 11), she saw a train of chariots full of distinguished people. Before she was aware of what she was doing her curiosity led her closer to look at this unusual sight. Hearing however the cries of admiration (*v.* 10), and abashed

---

[1] "Beautiful in elevation, a joy to all the land," Ps. xlviii. 3. "The perfection of beauty," Ps. l. 2. See Lam. ii. 15.

[2] The words לְבָנָה and חַמָּה are highly poetical. They occur Is. xxiv. 23—xxx. 26.

at being observed by the Court ladies, she turned to go away. She was however called back. "*Come back, Shulamite girl, let us look at you,*" they cried. "Why," she said, "what do you wish to look at in a country girl from Shulem, you Court-ladies from Jerusalem?" The reply came, "Something as graceful and beautiful *as the* celebrated *dance* of *Mahanaim,*" where, it may be presumed, as at Shiloh, sacred dances at yearly feasts and other popular assemblies took place[1]. Whether the allusion was to the solemn beauty of the ceremony, or to the grace and charm of the women who took part in it, is not clear. Perhaps both elements were combined in this praise. The reminiscence stops at this point but the rest has already been told in a very few words, "*The king has brought me into his apartments,*" i. 4.

(c) vii. 2—11. Twice has the Shulamite adjured the ladies of the harem not to endeavour to stir up or awaken in her a love for Solomon, ii. 7; iii. 5. In verses 2—7 of this picture the poet gives a vivid description of such an attempt. One of the inhabitants of the harem, in the presence it would seem of the king himself, delivers this audacious speech, which is evidently designed to set before the reader, in vivid colours, the contrast between the girl who breathes the degraded atmosphere of those unhappy surroundings, and the pure country maiden who is there against her will (see vi. 9). It is the crowning effort of the struggle, and Solomon has invoked to his aid this dubious ally to prepare the way for him. The Shulamite is addressed as the *daughter of a prince.* She spoke in vi. 12 of the *prince's retinue,* and the present expression implies that she now belongs to the household of that prince[2], is in fact one of the "daughters of Jerusalem." After sensuous and unpleasant allusions to *feet, thighs, navel* and *body,* the speech proceeds to praise of the *breasts* in a phrase already used in iv. 5 by Solomon; but the allusion to *lilies* is not repeated here as it has already been made in *v.* 3. Then the

---

[1] Mahanaim was an ancient sacred site, Gen. xxxii. 3; and a Levitical city, Josh. xxi. 39. For the yearly dances at Shiloh, Judges xxi. 19 f.; Ewald, *Ant. E. T.,* p. 285.

[2] The word בַּת frequently denotes that which belongs to or is dependent on any person or thing, 1 Sam. i. 16; Ezek. xxvii. 6; Eccl. xii. 4; Mal. ii. 11. So in this poem vi. 9, בָּנוֹת, of whom it is implied she is now become one.

neck in its shapely whiteness is compared to some well-known tower of ivory[1]. The *eyes* in their liquid splendour to twin pools at the gate of Heshbon. The *nose* is like a watch-tower built on the slopes of Lebanon and looking out towards Damascus[2]. The *head* with its *flowing locks* stands proudly erect like the headland of Carmel majestically looking out to sea and richly wooded[3], and in those flowing locks *a king is bound captive*. He whom all maidens love (i. 3) is your willing slave. Then, as if to point the conclusion of all this eulogy, follows the exclamation, *How delightful a thing is love*, and all its delights are offered to you by a king! *v.* 7. Solomon is not slow to proceed on the path thus indicated to him. This final attempt of his is very different in character, much more determined and direct than any of the preceding ones. The action of the piece has reached its height; the moment is decisive. So he expresses himself in terms that are quite unmistakable. *Thy commanding stature is like a palm tree and thy breasts its clusters of fruit;* my purpose is *to ascend the tree and grasp its branches.* I would enjoy the flavour and perfume of all thy precious fruits. To this passionate appeal there is no response. No praise of his has ever met an answering word. Once more he tries. Her kisses would be to him *like the best wine* (see i. 2).—She can bear no more and breaks in upon this speech. Such wine belongs only to *my beloved*. It is his by right and his *lips and teeth* alone will receive it. Then, leaving the figure, in one simple grave sentence she repels all the offers and flatteries she has for so long been obliged to listen to. *I belong to my beloved and he longs for me.* With these words the picture closes, but it is quite clear that the struggle is over, and this appears quite plainly from viii. 10, "I was like a walled city, the enemy could not take me—he realised this—and I obtained an honourable treaty of peace."

Note. The explanation of *vv.* 2—7 has caused many difficulties and much difference of opinion. Ewald and Ginsburg regarded them as spoken

[1] Compare the "ivory palaces," Ps. xlv. 9; Am. iii. 15. See 1 Kings xxii. 39; Burney's *Notes on Kings*, p. 259.

[2] David had placed military posts in 'Aram of Damascus,' which he had subjugated and made tributary, 2 Sam. viii. 6; and one of these garrisons may have been stationed on Antilibanus. See Kittel, *Gesch.* ii. 194.

[3] See Micah vii. 14.

by Solomon, but this is really out of the question. Even an Eastern poet could hardly picture him using some of the expressions contained in these verses.

Some interpreters abandoned the attempt to deal with the passage, regarding it as an interlude of some unexplained kind or an interpolation[1]. Others introduced another character to whom it was possible to think such words might be addressed (a harem-lady, Hitzig—a dancing girl, Renan, Adeney). Such a hypothesis is most unpleasing. It would be anything but good taste that the poet should introduce at the very crisis and deciding moment of the action of his story an unnecessary figure of this kind, contributing nothing to the development of the story, and only distracting the attention of the reader. The solution of the difficulty proposed above (which is that of Oettli) meets every necessity of the case. The poet has already, vi. 9, drawn the contrast between the pure Shulamite and the large company of corrupted women: it is part of his ethical purpose—and he develops it here. In that pernicious atmosphere and in the mouth of one of that tainted company a speech like this is not surprising. The flattering utterance, *A king is bound captive in thy tresses*, is quite suitable in the mouth of such a person, and the praise of *love, v.* 9, belongs to the same order of thought as i. 2—3, sung in the same place by similar voices.

(*d*) vii. 12—viii. 4. In this picture the Shulamite is just about to leave the palace, and the beloved is there to receive her. The Court ladies who wished to see him (v. 9) have now an opportunity to gratify their curiosity, and she herself can speak to him openly and without fear. She summons him to leave the city and travel with her through the country, *lodging in the villages* on the way until they reach Shulem. Arrived there, their first visit will be to the vineyards, the scenes of their former happiness (ii. 3, 4), and to see the progress of the opening spring, which she had been in quest of on a momentous occasion (vi. 11) and which he had described at their first stolen interview, ii. 8—17. *There,* in those happy scenes, redolent of sweet memories and far from these hateful surroundings, *I will give thee my caresses.* The *mandrakes,* emblems of love, grow there[2], we will enjoy their perfume, and there are *precious fruits*

---

[1] See Robertson Smith, *Enc. Brit.,* 9th ed., art. Canticles.

[2] These plants are common in Galilee, rare in Judæa. See Gen. xxx. 14—18. "In this passage the *fruit* is intended (at the time of the wheat-harvest, i.e. May to June) while in Song of Songs the *blossom* is meant (cf. the LXX. rendering in Song of Songs [vii. 14] οἱ μανδραγόραι with their translation here [Gen. xxx. 14] μῆλα μανδραγόρου)." Spurrell, *Notes on Genesis,* p. 234.

in my home *which I stored up for thee.* She cannot embrace him now, *as if he were a brother. She would be despised;* it is not seemly to kiss a betrothed one in public. But she longs as she longed in her dream (iii. 4) to *bring him to her mother's house.* May her mother be the witness of their innocent joys! She will not refuse her consent to their happy union. And she anticipates the pleasure of giving him a draught of home-made wine, prepared from the plants she has nurtured herself, viii. 1, 2. We breathe a different atmosphere here. The healthy tone of country life takes the place of the close, perfumed air of the royal apartments. There is not a trace of the influence of harem-life on this child of the northern farm and the open air. So, turning away for a moment from her lover to the Court ladies, the companions of her captivity, and the witnesses of her trials, she bids them farewell in the same words she had previously uttered to them in the very height of her trouble (ii. 6, 7), *Oh that his left hand were under my head and that his right hand did embrace me!* How differently those words sound now, in this happy juncture! Then for the last time comes the adjuration, formerly (ii. 7; iii. 5) a stern prohibition—now rather, by a slight change of expression, a rebuke and a warning: "You have seen, by all that has happened since I entered these doors, how vain have been your efforts to stir up in me any feeling for the king. Now you have seen how useless it has been in my case, and for the benefit of others in whom my experience may be repeated, I say for the last time, *Why will ye stir up and why awaken Love until it please* Love to wake?"

Canto V.

(*a*) viii. 5—12. The scene of this picture is at Shulem. The beloved and the Shulamite, leaning on his arm, are seen approaching from the country, having made the journey mentioned in vii. 12. As they reach her mother's home (see iii. 4; viii. 2) he points out to her an apple-tree where at the beginning of their acquaintance he waked her from sleep to love, *v.* 5. She answers him with a fine apostrophe as to the nature of true love, to which the whole poem has been leading up[1]—its

---

[1] "Der Verfasser hat die Sentenz in Bereitschaft, und durfte sie nicht mehr lange ausschieben." Hitzig.

climax and its moral. "Keep me," she says, "as your most
precious jewel, the *signet ring* you wear on your breast or your
hand[1]." Such is the love she would have and none other. For
love is as irresistible as *Death*, and as tenacious as *Hades* itself.
It seizes upon the beloved object and will not let him go. It
flashes as rapidly as the *lightning flash*[2], it burns as vehemently
as a fierce *fire flame*. No opposition can avail against it, no
floods or *torrents* can extinguish such a divine flame. What, to
such a love, are Solomon's bribes or flatteries? *If a man* (even
a king) *should give all the wealth of his house* to gain it, he
would only be an object of derision, *vv.* 6, 7. This is the love
which had given her the victory in her hard conflict, and this
is the love she expects in return. Next she recalls and quotes
some words of her brothers (see i. 6), spoken by them sometime before, when she was not yet quite grown up, but when
they felt the time approaching when they might be asked
for her hand in marriage[3]. "*If she be a wall*, resisting all
temptations, we will bestow on her suitable rewards, *but if she
be a door,* open and accessible to seductive proposals, we will
lock her up for safety." Which did I prove? she may ask
with pride. I proved a fortress *wall* with impregnable *towers*.
I resisted all attacks and all propositions of the enemy; he
recognized that he could not conquer me, and I obtained an
honourable treaty of peace, *vv.* 8—10. This thought leads her
to another. She had spoken of the hopelessness of a man who
would give all the wealth of his house for love. And how
wealthy was Solomon! One only of his possessions, a vineyard
not far from her home, at Baal Hamon, brought him in a
revenue of 1000 shekels yearly. But *I have a vineyard* too
(i. 6), equally precious to me, myself, my personal honour and
liberty. And I have kept it, *it is in my own power,* unsold,
unspoilt. Keep your vineyard, Solomon, with all its revenues,
but you shall not have mine! *v.* 11. With this light touch

---

[1] The signet was hung round the neck on a string, Gen. xxxviii. 16, or on
the right hand, Jer. xxii. 24, as a choice and precious possession, Hag. ii. 23.

[2] רֶשֶׁף or רִשְׁפֵי־חִץ. "Resheph of the arrows" was the name of a god
mentioned in Phoenician and N. Syrian inscriptions (Cook, *N. Sem. Ins.*,
Nos. 12 and 61, line 2). His name seems to have been used as equivalent to
lightning flashes—"Resheph's arrows." See Ps. lxxvi. 4. So "sparks" are
called בְּנֵי רֶשֶׁף, "sons of Resheph," Job v. 7.

[3] Comp. Gen. xxiv. 49, 50.

of scorn she dismisses the king from her thoughts and her life.

(b) *vv.* 13, 14. The poem closes with a charming little picture. The Shulamite is in her garden, and the beloved arrives with his companions (i. 7) and asks her to sing. The phrase he uses, *Let me hear thy voice,* reminds her vividly of a time of danger and distress when he used the same phrase, ii. 14. Things are very different now, and she playfully reminds him of that former time by repeating, almost verbally, what she then said as a serious caution, *Run away, my beloved, and be like a gazelle or a young hart on spicy mountains* (see ii. 17). Not now the *craggy mountains.* "These two expressions resume admirably the two opposite situations, and reveal a great poet. Nature, in fact, seems dark and sad to a sad heart; she appears bright and joyous to a joyous heart. The one only sees the rocks, the frightful precipices of the mountains; the other only perceives the aromatic perfumes of the meadows and the woods[1]." She does not really wish him to go, only to remind him of past sorrow in the light of present happiness. So in this hour of sunny brightness we take leave of our reunited pair of lovers.

11. THE INTERPRETATION OF THE POEM.

Reviewing the preceding analysis of the poem, the writer feels no inclination to minimise the great difficulty of interpreting it. An editor would indeed be sanguine who could hope that *all* the readings and renderings and explanations which he has adopted would command the assent of competent critics, especially in regard to a work which seems to have been written as if the object of its author had been to create differences of opinion. But upon one matter he feels no misgiving, viz. as to the soundness of the *method* he has laid down as the basis of his work. He is convinced that anyone who desires to understand and explain the Song ought to be guided by these principles :—

1. To interpret the work *as a whole,* using every part to explain every other part, and taking careful note of repetitions and variations of phrase.

---

[1] Bruston, *La Sulammite,* p. 44.

2. To interpret the work *as it stands*, and not, in the desire to maintain a theory, to make it into something else by conjectural emendation[1].

3. To interpret with as much *simplicity* as possible and to avoid elaborate and far-fetched theories based on slight indications.

4. To interpret without regard to *metrical theories*.

Whether the writer has been successful, or how far he has been successful, in the application of these principles, it will be for others to say—but he is fully satisfied that they are the only basis on which a satisfactory and enduring edifice of interpretation can be raised.

It has, however, been advanced that there is a general objection to the method of interpretation adopted in these pages, that the whole system, as well as the explanation of details, is a production of *modern* modes of thought[2]. And two instances are given.

(I) It is alleged that in all the East and in Israel, no woman had any say at all as to whom she wished to marry. The decision lay especially with the father, from whom the wife was usually bought; sometimes the brothers took part in the transaction. If the girl was asked for her consent it was only *pro forma,* as the matter had already been arranged. As regards Love, it usually came afterwards—in any case, as regarded the bride, it was not considered a matter of consequence. Love relations with intimate meetings passed as something quite unheard of.

So far as regards *marriage,* there is much force in this. There was undoubtedly a custom in Israel of buying a wife from her father or, if she had none, from her brothers—or of winning her by performing some service, acceptable to and appointed by them. The price paid, or service rendered, was known as *Mohar*[3]. It might be money (Gen. xxxiv. 12; Ex. xxii. 15, 16), or goods, or both (Hos. iii. 2), or farm service (Gen. xxix. 18), or, in relation to a king's daughter, service in

---

[1] Delitzsch remarks about Graetz's edition, "*This* Song is certainly not written by Solomon, nor yet does it date from the Syro-Macedonian time but was invented in Breslau in the 19th century of our era."

[2] Siegfried, p. 85.

[3] Ewald, *Ant. E. T.,* p. 200. Driver, *Notes on Samuel,* p. 119.

war (1 Sam. xviii. 23 f., where it is expressly said that no money price was required). But surely this need not imply that in no case were the feelings of the bride regarded as of any consequence, and that she was simply sold as a chattel; much less that there never was a previous inclination on her part, or mutual affection between the parties. To say that meetings of lovers, and affectionate relations between them, were unknown[1] is not only contrary to human nature and to all probability, but it is also opposed to such scanty evidence as is extant. *Jacob* meets Rachel at the well, makes her acquaintance and kisses her affectionately, and only after a residence of a month with her people was the question of *Mohar* discussed (Gen. xxix., see *v.* 18). Did he never meet Rachel during that month? *Dinah* wanders out alone and meets the young man Hamor in the fields. It is after the sad issue of these meetings that his father comes to Jacob, and offers for her an ample *Mohar* and gift (Gen. xxxiv. 12)[2]. *Samson* went down to Timnath and made the acquaintance of a Philistine girl, and then desired his father to arrange matters, and he went with his father and mother to see the girl again before the money arrangements were made (Jud. xiv. 8). *Michal*, the daughter of Saul, "fell in love with David," and when Saul knew of it, he then explained to David what his wishes were as to *Mohar* (1 Sam. xviii. 25). That this was a marriage of affection may well be inferred from the fact that after she had been forcibly taken from David (1 Sam. xxv. 44) he took considerable trouble to regain her (2 Sam. iii. 13). Indeed, that a period of betrothal could imply intimate and affectionate relations between the parties, may be seen from the beautiful passage where Jeremiah, reminding the nation of Israel (personified as a wife) of their early religious fervour, exclaims,

"I remember about thee, the kindness of thy youth,
The love of thy betrothal time" (Jer. ii. 2).

Such a phrase would have had no meaning if mutual endearments prior to marriage had been unknown to the people he was addressing.

---

[1] How, on this view, is legislation like Exod. xxii. 16, Deut. xxii. 28 to be understood?

[2] The מֹהַר or personal gift to the bride seems to have been an essential feature of a marriage contract. See Gen. xxiv. 53; Driver's *Com. on Gen.*, p. 237.

In view of these facts, can anyone pronounce it an impossible conception that, in the meadows and vineyards and wooded hills of Galilee, a youth and a maid should find opportunity to meet and exchange mutual vows of affection? They would be aware that, sooner or later, matters would have to be arranged with her relations, but that would not prevent their meeting.

Our poet shews himself to be perfectly alive to the prevalent Hebrew customs regarding marriage. The brothers of the Shulamite are represented as anxious to protect their sister from danger, so that they may obtain the customary *Mohar* when she is married (viii. 8, 9). When they find that she has made the acquaintance of a young man (viii. 1), and that there have been meetings in woodland resorts (i. 17; ii. 3), they are not unnaturally angry with her, and banish her into the vineyards (i. 5). But what, knowing all this, does the poem tell us of the girl's sentiments and desires? She would be willing to wander in search of her lover over the steppes where he feeds his flocks (i. 7). In her dreams she searches for him in the streets of the city (iii. 3; v. 6). She intends to walk home with him through the plain and lodge in the villages, and she hopes again to have tender meetings with him in the vineyards (vii. 12, 13). And she arrives at her home leaning on his arm (viii. 1). And the fine appeal for constancy and impassioned eulogy of love (viii. 6—8) is spoken by this unmarried woman to her lover at her own home. We need not doubt that the poet would have agreed that there could not and would not be any *marriage* till 'the beloved' had arranged *Mohar* with the brothers. But this is outside the scope and action of his poem. His theme is mutual affection and constancy before marriage. It may be "modern," but that cannot be helped.

(II) It is suggested that the conduct attributed to Solomon is also too *modern*. That when Eastern kings wanted a woman they did not court her long, they knew a shorter way (Gen. xii. 14, 15; xx. 2; 2 Sam. xi. 2—5). The references to Genesis are singularly inapt. In the three instances[1] mentioned in that

---

[1] " It is difficult to avoid suspecting that the three narratives (Gen. xii., xx., xxvi.) are variations of the same fundamental theme, a story told popularly of the Patriarchs and attributed sometimes to different occasions in the life of Abraham and once also to an occasion in the life of Isaac." Driver, *Com. on Gen.* p. 205. But to a Hebrew reader they would be three separate instances.

book the kings of Egypt and of Gerar did exactly what Solomon did in our poem. They brought a woman into the harem by force, and let her go again uninjured. And therefore these precedents are all in favour of our interpretation. But the real answer to this objection is that it fails to recognise the delicate touch with which our poet has drawn the character of the king. He is not thought of as a semi-savage chieftain, but as a courtly, luxurious, and rather elderly monarch with an enormous experience of women, a connoisseur in love-making. Such a man wants to succeed by his own fascinations; he is too much of an artist to resort to brutal violence. He would like to win the girl's affections, his own are not deeply engaged. And when he finds that presents, and compliments, and his personal charm, make no impression on her, and that she declares herself unalterably devoted to another—well, let her go, the king will find his consolation elsewhere. All girls love him (i. 3). This one, it appears, is an exception. Such is the character which the poet draws with a kind of good-natured scorn (viii. 7). He does not think of the king as a brutal ruffian who would resort to violence : he is a cultivated man, and besides, he has a religious[1] and ethical code which would restrain him from such an infamous proceeding. If such be the character which the poet ascribes to Solomon, there is really nothing in this objection to our mode of interpretation.

12. AUTHORSHIP.

It is now universally admitted, that in spite of the title affixed to this book by a later hand, *Solomon* could not have been its author. This holds good whatever view may be held as to its correct interpretation[2]. Indeed if the view of the poem be adopted which is expressed in the foregoing pages, such an authorship is absolutely inconceivable. Solomon would never have put on record his own defeat, or written a poem in

---

[1] " Schon die wahre religion in deren gemeinde Salômo stehen will, muss ihn vor einem solchen hier doppelten gräuel bewahren." Ewald, *Dichter* II. 410.

[2] "Die Überschrift nennt König Salomo als den Verfasser. Das ist ebensogut ausgeschlossen, wenn er als handelnde Person auftritt, wie wenn er als feststehende Vorbild des Reichthums, der Üppigkeit, der Königsherrlichkeit nur angezogen wird." Budde, p. XXI.

which he figures in an unfavourable light. The expressions in c. viii., "Men would surely scorn him," "Keep your thousand (shekels), Solomon," could never have been penned by this royal lover, conscious of an unusual and unwelcome repulse. He whom "innumerable girls love" (i. 3, vi. 8) would never have written a poem to shew that there was one girl who could not be induced to love him.

Dismissing, then, any view of Solomonic authorship, it is necessary to examine the poem itself to see what indications it affords as to the point of view from which it is written, and the class of person who is likely to have conceived the idea of it. The author, whoever he was, is eloquent in praise of true love and fidelity in love, of mutual, chaste and spontaneous affection, and, in contrast to this beautiful and ideal relation, he scorns the false and unreal *simulacrum* of love which is found in the harem of a polygamous king. In working out this idea, he centres his scorn and disapproval around the person of a king who in Hebrew literature generally stands for the ideal of all that is noble, wise, great, and distinguished. It is something of a strange phenomenon in that literature to find a writing which, while not detracting from the general picture of the glory and greatness of Solomon as found elsewhere, yet does venture to treat him with scorn and surround him with an atmosphere of satire. Somewhere in his realm there must have been a current of opinion which did not regard him with favour, to which his wealth, his luxurious court life, and his enormous harem were an unpleasing picture, to which the description of his repulse by a country girl from Galilee and her rustic lover afforded an exhilarating spectacle, and seemed to furnish suitable material for exhibiting the pompous Judean king in a ridiculous light. We shall hardly be wrong in tracing such a current of opinion in the traditional dislike of the Northern tribes to the hegemony of the house of David[1]. The kingdom of David was a union of tribes of diverse origin and varying qualities, and, in the earlier stages of national history, the tribe of Judah and those of the North had gone on their own separate lines of development with little connection or unity of purpose. Under the powerful hand of David the tribe of Judah sprang

[1] See the excellent remarks in Kittel, *Gesch. des V. Isr.* 2te Auf. Bd. II., p. 313 f. See also pp. 223—4.

to the head of the nation, but even his power and skill never succeeded in welding the tribes into a whole, or doing more than maintaining by force the unity of the nation. The long resistance of the North under Eshbaal at the beginning of David's reign (2 Sam. ii.—iv.) and the rebellion of Sheba ben Bichri towards its end (2 Sam. xx. 1—22) shewed only too plainly that the ten tribes of the North were not united to Judah by any inner bond of sentiment, and that the rule of the Judean kings was really to them a foreign rule. This feeling found utterance in the ominous watchword of Sheba,

> We have no portion in David,
> And we have no inheritance in Jesse's son,
> Every man to his tents, oh Israel !

which was to be fatally re-echoed at a later time (1 Kings xii. 16). The reign of Solomon, prosperous and successful as it appeared outwardly to be, did nothing to allay this smouldering hostility of the Northern tribes, or to bind Ephraim closer to the Davidic house. On the contrary there were many causes which tended to widen the breach. The king's Court pomp, costly buildings, and enormous harem involved a crushing burden of taxation, collected on a systematic basis by a host of officials (1 Kings iv. 7—19), and, what was more odious, the free tribes of the North found themselves forced to render the services of the *corvée*, and to give their personal labour to the public works of the Judean tyrant[1]. It was no accident that the standard of revolt was raised in Solomon's lifetime by a young Ephraimite whom the king had appointed as overseer of the forced labour of his fellow-tribesmen (1 Kings xi. 28). Jeroboam was thus placed in a position to hear the complaints and to witness the sufferings of "the house of Joseph" condemned to this hateful slavery, and this specific cause of discontent was added to the old aversion of the Northern tribes against the house of David. The refusal of Solomon's successor to abolish the *corvée* and oppressive taxation gave the impulse to the Northern tribes to make a final breach with the house of David (1 Kings xii. 4—16), and it was thus the luxury, extravagance and wantonness of Solomon which contributed largely to free the Northern

---

[1] That this was so notwithstanding 1 Kings ix. 22 appears from 1 Kings iv. 7, v. 27, xi. 28, xii. 3 f. See Ewald, *Gesch. E. T.* III. 230 and note 2.

tribes from their unwilling allegiance to the Judean monarchy and make Jeroboam the king of Israel.

But the separation was not only due to *political* but to *religious* causes. The Northern tribes contained many sacred sites, with traditions of theophanies and patriarchal worship, and with temples frequented by many worshippers and the seats of powerful and influential priestly bodies. The shrines of Shiloh, Shechem, Bethel, Dan, and others had long traditions of sanctity, and for a considerable period the priesthood of Shiloh had virtually governed the confederacy of the tribes of Israel (1 Sam. ii.). The choice of Jerusalem as the capital of the realm and the erection of the temple there must have been very distasteful to the votaries of these old-Israelite shrines. It portended a centralisation of worship which must ultimately deal a death blow at these venerable seats of worship, abolish the wealth and influence of their priestly dignitaries, and divert their streams of pilgrims to Jerusalem, making that city the undisputed metropolis of Church and State. It was with a clear consciousness of this danger to his young kingdom that Jeroboam as one of his first public actions restored the old sanctuaries in Dan and Bethel to cut off the stream of pilgrims resorting to Jerusalem (1 Kings xii. 26 fol.). Nor must it be forgotten that the first insurrection of Jeroboam was instigated by Ahijah, a prophet *of Shiloh* (1 Kings xi. 29), and that Rehoboam was restrained from his design of reconquering the revolted tribes by another prophet, Shemaiah (1 Kings xii. 23). The whole situation has been well summed up as follows: "The kingdom of Solomon was an innovation on old traditions, partly for good and partly for evil. But novelties of progress and novelties of corruption were alike distasteful to the north, which had long been proud of its loyalty to the principles of the good old times (2 Sam. xx. 18, 19). The conservative revolution of Jeroboam was in great measure the work of the prophets, and must therefore have carried with it the religious and moral convictions of the people[1]." A poet with these North country prejudices, disliking the Davidic dynasty, objecting to Solomon as a religious innovator, and as the proprietor of a large harem, is just the kind of man we may reasonably think of as the author of this song in which the daughter of the tribe of

[1] Robertson Smith in *Enc. Brit.* 9th ed. art. "Canticles."

Issachar triumphs over the polygamous king of the house of Judah.

Several other traits in the poem tend to confirm this view that the author belonged to the Northern kingdom[1]. It is easy to understand how a poet of that kingdom should put in the same rank the little capital of Tirzah and Jerusalem, which no Judean poet would have thought of doing. The description of the harem as "daughters of Jerusalem" does not suggest a Judean author. The fact that the Song was known to Hosea[2], the North country prophet, suggests that the two authors were fellow-countrymen, and it was in the North that some of the finest early Hebrew poetry, the Song of Deborah, the prophecies of Hosea, the 45th Psalm, had their origin. "The beauties of nature in this country of Lebanon, an agricultural land, wonderfully fertile, rich in woods, prairies and flowing streams, were more fitted to inspire pastoral poetry than the sandy, stony districts of the South." And further, with the exception of Jerusalem and En-gedi, every locality mentioned by the poet "in a manner which usually shews him to have been personally familiar with them"[3] is situate in the kingdom of the Ten Tribes. He knows Sharon, Bether (if this be a proper name), Lebanon (often mentioned), Gilead, Hermon (of which he knows the Amorite name, Senir, and the Assyrian name, Amana), Tirzah, Mahanaim, Heshbon, Bathrabbim, the Tower of Lebanon looking out towards Damascus, Carmel, Baal-Hamon, and, finally, his heroine is of Sulem. All these places are named by him with some suitable trait—the goats coming down the slopes of Gilead, the panthers in Hermon, the dance of Mahanaim, the twin pools of Heshbon—and the poem as a whole has a north-country flavour, like the undoubted north-country poems we have named above. Budde seems to have missed the point when he objects that Heshbon was not in the North[4]. Quite true, it was in the same latitude as Jerusalem.

[1] See Renan, pp. 112—14.
[2] See Excursus IV.
[3] Driver, *Introd.* 1st ed. 421.
[4] "Wo zeigt sich denn der Verf. so wohlvertraut mit nordisraelitischen Örtlichkeiten...Die Namen einer Anzahl von Gebirgen die jeder kannte [does any other writer mention Amana?] und eine Stadt...das ist alles. Dem stehn Engedi, Saron (?), Hesbon, Kedar gegenüber, die nach dem Süden verweisen," p. XXII.

But, and this is what is material, it belonged to the Northern kingdom, it was in Gilead. The poet describes places in the realm to which he belongs, and his fancy does not stray; perhaps his travels had not led him much into Judah. The only place he mentions in that tribe, En-gedi, is referred to in connection with the henna-flower (i. 14), which appears to have grown there, and nowhere else. But his geographical outlook, like that of the Song of Deborah or of Hosea, is that of the kingdom of the Ten Tribes.

Now if this be a correct view of the author, if his outlook is mostly towards Lebanon and Hermon and the country dominated by them, and if his feelings and prejudices are those of a North Israelite, it is not difficult to realise the impression which the story of the Shulamite girl would make upon him. The story had probably some basis of fact, and the fact was such as to set the poet on fire. It assailed every prejudice. That the Judean king, in violation of religion and good old manners, should take this Northern girl into a harem, which was itself an offence to every Northern heart—here was stuff for a poem, which should exhibit this luxurious and wanton king repulsed and scorned in favour of an humble, but faithful Northern farmer. The genius of the poet added to this simple theme all the movement and colour, the lovely description of natural objects, and the fine delineation of true love, as well as the darker shades of a polygamous court—and the story of the maid of Shulem became a masterpiece of national poetry, which would be dear to every patriotic heart.

Such we conceive to have been the genesis of this poem, but there is another view which of late years has received a good deal of support. It is supposed that the designation "Shulamite" refers to Abishag of Shunem, whose history is found in 1 Kings i. 3, 15; ii. 17, 21. She was the most beautiful girl in all Israel, and it is suggested that "the girl from Shulem" was a proverbial expression for "the most beautiful woman," and was so used by the women guests at the (Syrian?) wedding ceremony as equivalent to "the fairest among women" (i. 8, &c.)[1]. This is part of the same system of make-believe which turns the Song into a bundle of ballads sung at a

[1] Budde, p. 36; Siegfried, p. 88; Cheyne, in *Enc. Bib.* art. "Song of Solomon," and see § 9 *sup*.

wedding, by making every expression mean something different from its natural meaning. "Shulamite" means "a woman whose home is at Shulem," and we need not look for artificial or secondary meanings, nor is there any evidence that "Shunamite" was a proverbial expression for "beautiful." In fact in the only other places where it occurs (2 Kings iv. 12, 25, 36) it has obviously no such implication, but is used, as in the Song, simply as a Gentile noun.

This theory has however been stated in a more reasonable form as follows. In 1 Kings ii. we hear nothing of Abishag having really become the wife of Solomon. Why may not this circumstance have given rise in poetic legend to the conception that the lovely virgin *refused* to become Solomon's wife—nay even to the conception that her refusal was based upon her unconquerable love for a youth in her native district? Moreover, when the notion was once seized that she had not chosen to be the wife of Solomon, it was no great stretch of poetic fancy to assume that her first introduction into the apartments of David was not a willing one on her part, and the presupposition that from the first she succeeded in defending her honour finds its firm basis in the express statement of 1 Kings i. 4, "and the king knew her not[1]." This is quite possible, though rather artificial and far-fetched, and it is quite in harmony with the views above suggested as to the character and sentiments of the author. But on the other hand there are many difficulties about accepting it. If the story of Abishag is really the basis of the Song, it is hard to see why the author has departed so widely from it. There is no mention of David or of the ignoble service which this Shunamite girl was compelled to render to him, and there is no evidence in Kings that this poor girl was ever released from the harem. More probably (see Esth. ii. 14) she would have the unhappy lot of becoming a permanent inmate there. And surely if the poem had been written about Abishag, her name would have been given.

It is on the whole more likely that the story which reached our author referred to another girl from Shulem whose name is not given by him *because he did not know it* (which may also have been the case with the author of 2 Kings iv.), and that he

---

[1] Rothstein, *Hastings Bib. Dict.* IV. 593.

embodied in his poem the main outlines of this story, as popular legend had expressed them, and with the feelings and prejudices which such a story was bound to arouse in North Israel.

13. DATE.

To ascertain the date at which this poem was composed regard must be paid not only to what has been said in the preceding section as to the situation and sentiments of the author, but to any other indications which may be gathered from the poem itself, taken in connection with general history. It should then be observed:

(a) This poem "retained a definite historical remembrance of all the peculiarities of the age of Solomon, and was flooded by a most copious stream of genuine popular recollections of David and Solomon[1]." It alludes, e.g., to Solomon's favourite mare in the chariots he had obtained from Pharaoh, i. 9, to his vineyards at En-gedi, i. 14, his state litter, iii. 7, his body-guard of *gibborim*, who are otherwise never heard of after the time of David, *ib.*, his regal crown, iii. 10, David's tower and the shields hung on it, iv. 4, Solomon's harem, vi. 8 (which must be an independent tradition, the numbers in 1 Kings xi. 3 being so different), the tower in Lebanon, vii. 5, Solomon's vineyard in Baal-Hamon and his arrangements with his tenants, viii. 11, 12. Some, but by no means all, of these traits might possibly have been gleaned by a zealous antiquary of later days from notices in 1 Kings, but the allusive way in which they are introduced without explanation or dissertation rather serves to suggest that they came to the author either by personal observation or popular tradition, that they were, so to speak, in the air when he wrote, and that the book was composed near enough to the time of Solomon for such matters to be still remembered. How would a writer in Judea, centuries after, have known what sum Solomon paid to the keepers of his vineyard in North Israel, or what annual revenue he derived from it?

(b) The delineation in the poem of the life and occupations of simple people, farmers and vineyard owners in North Israel, slight as it is, gives a general impression not only of brightness and cheerfulness, but of prosperity and peace. There is no sign

---

[1] Ewald, *Gesch. E. T.* IV. 42. Comp. Renan, pp. 97 fol.

of war or foreign invasion in the happy picture. The shepherd
wanders with his flocks far and wide over the open country,
i. 7, 8, a girl may, alone, keep the vineyards, i. 5, there are stores
of provision in the farm house, vii. 14, and country wines, viii. 2.
The country folk take pleasant walks, ii. 3, and there is singing
in the land, ii. 12, viii. 13, and throughout, blooming vineyards
and fruit trees fill the picture. It is not the description of a
country devastated by marauding bands or hostile armies.
Such a picture could hardly have been drawn after the 12th
year of the reign of Baasha[1] when, at the request of Asa of
Judah, Benhadad of Damascus invaded the territories of Baasha
with a large force and took "Ijon, and Dan, and Abel-beth-
Maachah, and all Chinneroth, with all the land of Naphthali"
(1 Kings xv. 20). From that time began the unhappy series
of Syrian wars and raids which perpetually sucked out the
life-blood of North Israel and menaced its tranquillity. It must
have been in the happy days before this invasion that our poet
could write this joyous picture of a people who might well be
described in the language of another old poem:

> "Our sons are as plants
> Full grown in their youth;
> Our daughters like corners
> Meetly polished for a temple building;
> Our barns are full,
> Supplying all kinds of stores;
> Our sheep bring forth thousands
> And tens of thousands in our fields;
> Our oxen bravely bear the yoke,
> No breaking in (of foes), no marching forth (to war),
> And no cry of woe in our streets." (Ps. cxliv. 12—14.)

(c) On the other hand, the feelings which our poem reveals
with regard to the Davidic house, and the scorn and dislike
which a North Israelite felt in relation to it, belong to the
period of the disruption or shortly after it, and could hardly
have survived the period when the royal houses of the two
kingdoms were in close alliance. As has been well observed,
"The unbroken continuous strife of brothers which had, as it
seems, gone on since Jeroboam's rebellion between Israel and
Judah, was brought to rest. What had earlier been long required

[1] For this date see 2 Chr. xvi. 1. Ewald, *Gesch. E. T.* IV. 34.

by prudence and national honour, since it became apparent that Rehoboam was not in a position to restore the lost unity by force, now took place. Jehoshaphat of Judah, Asa's successor, is the first king of Judah who is able to decide to accept as a settled thing the situation as it had shaped itself since Solomon's death. Not only is peace concluded, but the good understanding which now begins is sealed through the alliance of the two neighbouring dynasties. Jehoshaphat's son Joram marries Ahab's daughter Ataliah[1]." It is difficult to think that when such a marriage as this had taken place, or even when it was in contemplation, the feeling of scorn and bitterness towards the Davidic house could have continued to be operative. By that time the memory of Solomon's taxations and *corvées*, his novelties in religion and his polygamous excesses would have grown dim: other questions had taken their place—Syrian wars, Baal worship, Tyrian marriages. We therefore conclude that the composition of the Song, reflecting, as it does, the feelings of an earlier period, must have been considerably earlier than the reign of Ahab over Israel.

(*d*) There is however one passage in the Song which enables its date to be fixed with even greater precision, namely the phrase

> Thou art fair, my friend, as Tirzah,
> Comely as Jerusalem. (vi. 4.)

This passage is so important that its exact force must be carefully examined[2]. Tirzah was an old Canaanite city (Josh. xii. 24), but its only importance in history arose from the fact that it was for a brief period the residence of the early Israelite kings. Jeroboam appears to have at one time lived there (1 Kings xiv. 17), Baasha made it the royal residence (1 Kings xv. 33, see 21) and was buried there (1 Kings xvi. 6). Elah his son also lived there and was murdered there while at a banquet by Zimri (1 Kings xvi. 8—10). The latter reigned there seven days but being besieged by Omri burnt the royal palace over his own head and perished in the flames (1 Kings xvi. 15—20). Omri kept Tirzah as the capital six years longer (*ib., v.* 23), and then made Samaria the capital instead. Tirzah appears again

---

[1] Kittel, *Gesch.* II. 342.

[2] See on this subject Ewald, *Dichter* II. 339; *Gesch. E. T.* IV. 34; Hitzig, p. 10; Renan, p. 95; Kittel, *Gesch.* II. 388, n. 5.

as a fortress in the time of Menahem (2 Kings xv. 14—17), but is not further mentioned, and seems to have fallen into utter oblivion. The whole period of its existence as a capital with a royal palace would be from B.C. 914 to 889[1], 26 years, and this was the only period in which it could fairly be compared with Jerusalem.

Now it is obviously the purpose of the writer, whose views and feelings as a citizen of the Northern kingdom have been considered above, to put Tirzah on a level with Jerusalem. David had made Jerusalem the capital, and Solomon had built there a fine palace. The author, in his patriotic pride, feels and desires to express his satisfaction, that the young kingdom of the House of Joseph has also its dynasty, and its capital adorned with a royal palace, and to his mind the Northern capital is as fair as the Southern. Such a point of view is perfectly natural to that author, just at that epoch; it is inconceivable in any other writer at any other epoch. It had no force before Baasha made Tirzah his capital, or after Zimri burnt down the palace. The couplet in question could only have been written by a Northern poet within the fixed period of 26 years.

Conclusive as this appears to be, it has been contested by Budde as being inconsistent with the late date which he assigns to the poem. He remarks[2], "If a second Israelite capital was really sought for at a later period, this much is certain that no one would choose Samaria, which gave its name to the heretical Samaritans. It was easy to dig up the forgotten Tirzah out of the sacred books, all the more because the name of itself possessed a meaning (from רָצָה) which was excellently suited to the idea of beauty[3]." But why should a Jewish poet in the Greek age be seeking for a second Israelite capital at all, to

---

[1] According to Kittel, II. 308. Wellhausen, *Gesch.* 5te Ausg. p. 74, puts the accession of Omri about 900, some 10 years earlier. Both writers correct the Bible chronology by the Assyrian. Of course in Omri's period the palace was a burnt ruin, and his six years are therefore not to be taken into account.

[2] P. xxiii. In another place, p. 31, he resorts to his usual expedient in case of difficulty. "The words 'as Tirzah comely as Jerusalem' are not original"!! If so, what editor would be likely to insert them?

[3] "Die Wahl des Namens Tirzah erklärt sich nicht bloss aus einer Zeit in der diese Stadt wirklich eine Residenz war, denn man kannte die einstige Bedeutung des Ortes auch später noch aus dem Königsbuch." Steuernagel, *Lehrbuch*, sect. 161.

adorn his poem? He was under no obligation, and certainly would be driven by no inner impulse, to bring in the name of any Northern town as a rival to Jerusalem. To him Jerusalem was the loveliest spot on earth (Ps. xlviii. 2; Lam. ii. 15). Yahveh loved the gates of Zion more than all the dwellings of Jacob (Ps. lxxxvii. 2). It is difficult to imagine anything more unlikely than a Jewish writer in 200 B.C. quarrying in the sacred books to see if perchance he could dig up some city in the schismatic North worthy to be compared to the lovely, holy, unique Jerusalem, and all to give his poem a quite unnecessary ornament. It may be conceded that he was not likely to choose Samaria, but was Tirzah any better? the residence of the first schismatic king "who made Israel sin" and of others who followed in his footsteps? No Judean poet could have written this couplet, it is utterly outside his possible range of thought. Further, in the Greek age Tirzah was so utterly forgotten that not only the LXX. translator of the Song but all the other early Greek translators do not know that it is a proper name and translate it εὐδοκία or some similar form[1], from which fact it may reasonably be assumed that the supposed late Judean author would be similarly ignorant about this vanished city.

If the Song was written late, in post-exilic Judah, it is most difficult if not impossible to account for the coupling of Tirzah with Jerusalem as equal in beauty; if the Song was written early, in Israel, this phenomenon is natural and appropriate, and just what might be expected in view of the events of the period and the sentiments of the author. As a finishing touch, the delicate satirical stroke may be noted which puts this eulogy of the new Israelitish capital in the mouth of the hated Judean king. *Solomon* praises Tirzah as he praises his own capital.

From these various indications considered together it is a reasonable conclusion that the Song was written somewhere between the 1st and the 12th years of the reign of Baasha 914—902 B.C.

There are other indications in the poem which, though more general than those already referred to, all tend to support the view that the composition was early and pro-exilic.

---

[1] Aq. κατ᾽ εὐδοκίαν. Sym. εὐδοκήτη. Theod. and E[1] εὐδοκῶ. Gr. Venet. alone Τιρεσά.

It has been already observed that the poet speaks of many
places as if he was familiar with them and, it may be added
here, not as if they had ceased to belong to Israel by foreign
conquest, for in that event he was not likely to have visited
them. Thus he evidently knows *Heshbon.* Now Moab was
lost to Israel by the middle of Ahab's reign and Heshbon
according to an old oracle, preserved by Isaiah but much older
than his time, had long ceased to belong to Israel[1]. The Song
was probably written before this loss. Again he certainly knew
Gilead and *Mahanaim,* and the Song in all probability was
written before Tiglath Pileser in 734 conquered all the Trans-
jordanic provinces of Israel and deported all their inhabitants,
and extended the same treatment to "Galilee and all the land
of Naphthali," which expression would probably include other
localities named in the Song[2]. It might be suggested that these
names were collected and inserted in the poem by a Judean
antiquary in search of local colour, but the natural and lifelike
way in which they appear gives rather the impression that the
author had gazed on the flocks of goats moving down the slopes
of Gilead, and watched the dances at Mahanaim, in the happy
days of peace, before the terrible Assyrian power fell upon the
land: and if, as the writer believes, the prophet Hosea had read
the Song[3], this would be another proof that it was written before
734, for, in the time of this prophet, Gilead still belonged to
Israel (Hos. vi. 8; xii. 12).

Examining all these indications of date it may be declared
that few ancient writings express more clearly upon the face
of them the date of their composition than does this poem. In
fact the only serious objections which can be raised to the
suggested date are on the ground of *language.* This subject
has been fully examined elsewhere[4] and the writer will content
himself with stating here that he considers the late date suggested
(viz. cir. 240 B.C.) by Graetz and others as out of the question.
None of the writers who in recent times have advocated so late

---

[1] See line 8 of the Mesha Stone (in Driver on Sam. p. xxxviii); Is. xv. 4;
Jer. xlviii. 4; Cheyne's *Prophecies of Isaiah,* I. 96.

[2] See 2 Kings xv. 29; 1 Chron. v. 26; Schrader, *Die Keil-Inschrift. u. das
A. T.,* 2nd Ed. pp. 255—9; Maspero, *Hist. Anc.* III. 186.

[3] See Excursus IV.

[4] Excursus I and III *post.*

a date, have been able to maintain it without removing the most characteristic features of the poem by most extensive conjectural emendation[1]. Indeed, as regards *any* post-exilic date, the linguistic proofs adduced are far too precarious to outweigh the indications of date found in the matter of the poem.

14. THE SONG IN THE CANON.

The process by which the three divisions of the Hebrew Scriptures, the *Law*, the *Prophets*, and the *Writings*, obtained recognition as a separate and sacred Canon is very obscure, and has led to much conjecture and an extensive literature. It would be quite unsuitable to discuss this large question here, and all that it is proposed to do, is to draw attention to a few points relating to the third division of the sacred books [כְּתוּבִים, Hagiographa] and to the inclusion of Canticles as part of this third division in the Canon.

The materials are scanty, and what is extant is not all of equal value. The tradition that the Sacred Books were burnt by the Chaldeans and that Ezra rewrote them all by inspiration and added 70 more which he did not publish[2] can hardly be taken seriously, and the statement that Judas Maccabeus gathered together all those writings that were scattered by reason of the war in his time[3] is uncertain in its meaning, though it may well imply that some if not all of the Hagiographa were gathered together in his time[4]. In one of the Talmudic treatises however an authentic and important tradition seems to be preserved. When it is stated[5] "Hezekiah and his company wrote Isaiah, Proverbs, Song of Songs and Ecclesiastes" we are at once reminded of the statement in Prov. xxv. 1, "These, too, are Proverbs of Solomon, which men of Hezekiah king of Judah collected." These two statements seem to preserve the memory of a fact that in the time of Hezekiah a company or college of learned men existed, of whom Isaiah was one, and

---

[1] See § 9 *sup.* and Excursus II.

[2] 2 Esdras xiv. 19—48; Ryle on the *Canon*, Excursus A, p. 250 f. 2nd ed.

[3] 2 Macc. ii. 14.

[4] See Davidson on the *Canon*, p. 28; Ryle, p. 136.

[5] *Baba Bathra* I. 5 in Rodkinson's *Babyl. Talmud*, Vol. 5 (13), p. 45. See Ewald, *Dichter* II. 55, 353—5; Davidson, p. 42; Ryle, Excursus B, p. 290; Delitzsch, *Com.* p. 14.

that one of the principal literary activities of this college was to collect writings attributed to Solomon. In doing so they came upon the Song of Songs, which by this time had been provided with its title by an unknown hand, and they placed it in their collection as a genuine work of the great Jewish king. It was thus preserved in safety; perhaps for a time after the fall of the northern kingdom it was not much read, and it probably owed its reception at a later date into the third Canon, "the writings," to the fact that it was found in the archives of Judah and bore the honoured name of Solomon.

The first clear recognition of the existence of the "writings" as a third Canon appears in the Prologue to "The wisdom of Jesus the son of Sirach" (Ecclesiasticus), prefixed to the Greek translation of this book made by the author's grandson in Egypt in B.C. 130. In this preface[1] after remarking that "many and great things have been delivered to us by the law and the prophets and by the others who followed their steps" (καὶ τῶν ἄλλων τῶν κατ᾽ αὐτοὺς ἠκολουθηκότων), he states that his grandfather, "when he had much given himself to the reading of the law and the prophets and the other books of the fathers" (τῶν ἄλλων πατρίων βιβλίων), was drawn on to write something himself; and speaking of Greek translation he observes "that the law itself and the prophets and the rest of the books (τὰ λοιπὰ τῶν βιβλίων) have no small difference when they are spoken in their own language." The expressions quoted make it quite clear that in the time of this writer there was a third Canon of sacred books, worthy to be classed with the law and the prophets, and, like them, to be read and venerated, and which had, like them, been translated into Greek. They are "the books"—something well known to his readers, and the expressions he uses, though somewhat vague, are no more so than the word "writings" by which they were afterwards known. In fact the very varied nature of the books in this third group made it impossible to describe them by a more precise designation.

There has been much difference of opinion as to whether this third group in 130 B.C. contained the whole of the Hagiographa as we have them, whether in fact the third Canon was

---

[1] The original in Ryle, Excursus D, III.

then closed[1]. The author's words do seem to lead to this conclusion. The "rest of the books" cannot mean "the extant remains of Hebrew literature." It must mean something more definite than that—some books which form the remainder of a definite total when "the law" and "the prophets" have been already mentioned[2]. There is nothing to suggest that the third division is in course of formation, or that any addition could be made to it. It is something known, and settled, and marked by the definite article, a collection of which he could assert that his grandfather had read the whole, that the whole was known to his readers and had been translated into Greek. The other phrase, "the books of the fathers," indicates even more definitely the author's view that the list of sacred books was closed. It shews that the criterion by which the reception of books into the Sacred Canon was decided, was their supposed *antiquity*. They were books "of the fathers" belonging, as was believed, to the days before inspiration had ceased. It was the mournful belief of later Israel "that after the latter prophets Haggai, Zechariah and Malachi the Holy Spirit departed from Israel[3]," and the lament is frequent that there were no more prophets[4]. It was not possible that any books known to be composed after the date of the post-exilic prophets would be accepted as sacred. The Canon must necessarily be closed, because there could in the nature of things be no more old books to insert in "the writings"; and this, no doubt, is the reason why such books as Wisdom, Sirach, and 1 Maccabees never obtained Canonical rank, though many might think with Luther[5] that they were more suitable than Esther to form parts of Holy Scripture. But they were too late in date, and this was fatal to their claims.

But whatever books were included in the third Canon in 130 B.C. there can be no doubt the *Song* was one. The very

---

[1] See Bloch, *Studien zur Geschichte der Sammlung der alt. heb. Literatur*, pp. 132—60; Davidson, p. 32; Robertson Smith, *The O. T. in the Jewish Church*, p. 166; Green, *Gen. Introd. to O. T.* pp. 111—13; Buhl, *Canon and Text*, E. T. p. 14; Ryle, pp. 153—4; Budde, *Enc. Bib.* Art. *Canon*, Sec. 49.

[2] The words αἱ λοιπαί are used just in this way by Josephus, *C. Ap.* i. 8.

[3] Tract *Sanhedrin* quoted by Green, p. 39.

[4] 1 Macc. iv. 46, ix. 27, xiv. 41; Sirach xxxvi. 15; Song of the Three Children, 14.

[5] Davidson, p. 170.

peculiar nature of its contents, and the controversies which arose in regard to it at a later time, render it quite certain that such a book could never have been regarded as Holy Scripture, unless it had come down from a distant past and borne the honourable name of Solomon. Had it been written in the Greek age, its claims would have been infinitely less than those of Wisdom or Sirach. "That it was only at a very late period received into the collection is not only not supported by historical evidence, but is in itself a wholly unhistorical statement. More than for any other single writing must we for this very book presuppose an early currency and general favour. Otherwise it would certainly never have occurred to any Pharisee to regard it as canonical. That it could maintain its place was undoubtedly owing to the allegorical interpretation, whether suggested by R. Akiba or by someone else. But, on the other side, the attacks on its canonicity seem plainly to show that this allegorical interpretation was not generally accepted, and so there remains at least the possibility that in earlier times, under a simpler understanding of it, it had secured in the community its wide circulation[1]."

With these views the later testimony of Josephus (cir. 100 A.D.) is in entire accord. He says, "We have not an innumerable multitude of books among us, but only twenty-two books which contain the records of all the past times, which are justly believed to be Divine. And of them five belong to Moses.... But as to the time from the death of Moses till the reign of Artaxerxes king of Persia the prophets who were after Moses wrote down what was done in their time in thirteen books. The remaining four books contain hymns to God and precepts for the conduct of human life. It is true our history has been written since Artaxerxes very particularly, but has not been esteemed of the like authority with the former by our forefathers, because there has not been an exact succession of prophets since that time; and how firmly we have given credit to these books of our own nation is evident by what we do, for during so many ages as have already passed, no one has been so bold as either to add anything to them, to take anything from them, or to make any change in them; but it has become natural to all Jews, immediately and from their very birth, to

[1] Buhl, *Canon and Text*, E. T. p. 75.

esteem these books to contain Divine doctrines, and to persist in them, and, if occasion be, willingly to die for them[1]." It may be affirmed with practical certainty that the twenty-two books of Josephus are those of our present Hebrew Canon. The "hymns to God" are the Psalms and the Song of Songs, and the "precepts of life" Proverbs and Ecclesiastes. It is clear from these expressions that the Song must have been taken allegorically[2].

Josephus then, expressing the views of the Jews of his period, was of opinion (a) that the twenty-two books of his Canon were a separate collection of Divine origin, (b) that they were all ancient, that none were more recent than Artaxerxes, and that all had long been regarded as canonical, (c) that during many ages no book had been added to them. As with the grandson of Sirach, *antiquity* was the test of *canonicity*, and there was no thought of admitting into the Canon a book which was known to be of a later origin than the date of the supposed cessation of prophecy.

If these were the views of Josephus, and if in accordance with them he included the Song of Songs in the Canon as a "hymn to God," inspired, universally esteemed, a book to die for, such a view is easy to account for if the Song was really an old book, preserved along with part of Proverbs in Jewish archives since the days of Hezekiah. The tradition of antiquity and the name of Solomon would prevail over the undoubted difficulty arising from the very peculiar nature of its contents. But if the book was known to be of very late origin, and to be made up of ballads which everybody knew, because some of them were sung at every wedding; if the book itself was the libretto of a popular Wedding Cantata[3], then having regard to its contents[4], the reception of such a book into the Canon was simply impossible. How in the world could a company of learned Pharisees consider a book worthy

[1] Jos. *C. Apion*, I. 8, trans. by Davidson, p. 34; orig. in Ryle, Excursus D. VIII. p. 297.

[2] See Robertson Smith, *op. cit.* pp. 149—50; Ryle, p. 176.

[3] "Besitzen wir in den Hohenlied das Textbuch einer palästinisch-israelitischen Hochzeit," Budde, p. xix.

[4] "He who sings the Song of Songs in wine-shops and makes it into a (profane) song, has no share in the life to come" was a rabbinical prohibition. Tract *Sanhedrin*, quoted by Budde, p. x.

to be added to the Sacred Scriptures, when any one of them may well have heard it sung at his own wedding? And if the late date of Wisdom and Sirach was fatal to the reception of those pious and edifying books into the Canon, such a reason would be far stronger in the case of the Song. Nothing but a tradition of venerable antiquity, dating from ages before the time of Artaxerxes, could have given this particular book a chance of entry into the Canon.

It is somewhat curious that Josephus should have asserted with so much confidence that no one had ever sought to remove any book from the Sacred Canon, while other Jewish authorities reveal some curious discussions which had taken place on this subject shortly before he wrote. Probably he never heard of them, as they were merely "scholastic controversies which affected the public in a very slight degree[1]," and were largely logomachies between the rival schools of Hillel and Shamai[2]. The discussions principally arose as to whether certain books found in the Canon were rightfully there, in Rabbinical phrase whether they "defiled the hands." In order to preserve the Scriptures from profane or careless handling it was the rule that to touch them caused ceremonial defilement, and therefore to say that a book "defiled the hands" was equivalent to saying that it was Canonical Scripture. The books about which difficulties were felt were principally those attributed to Solomon. Thus we read in one place, "Formerly it was said, The Books of Proverbs, Song of Songs and Ecclesiastes were hidden (גנוזים, withdrawn, of disputed canonicity), and do not belong to the Hagiographa; the men of the Great Synagogue however came and explained them[3]," which seems to embody a tradition we shall find in a more detailed form later on. And again, "The book Ecclesiastes does not according to Beth Shamai render unclean the hands, while it does so according to Beth Hillel[4]."

This controversy came to a head and was finally disposed

---

[1] Buhl, *Canon and Text*, p. 27.

[2] "Why are the theories of Shamai and Hillel stated at all, if without avail? To teach to posterity that one must not insist on one's statements, since the distinguished masters of the world did not insist on their views." Tract *Eduyoth*, 1. 4 in Rodkinson, Vol. 9 (17), p. 6.

[3] *Aboth R. Nathan*, Rodkinson, Vol. 1, p. 3.

[4] *Eduyoth*, 5. 3, *ubi sup.*, note 2, p. 18.

of at a memorable assembly of the Jewish Church. After the fall of Jerusalem, the authority of the Sanhedrin was, to some extent, assumed by the great school of Jamnia (near Joppa), which became the headquarters of the Jews who remained in Palestine. An assembly of this school met in the year 90 A.D. for no less important a purpose than to depose its President Gamaliel, a proud and overbearing man, and to elect the youthful Eleazer in his place[1]. At this assembly a discussion took place as to the canonicity of the Song, of which a lively account is preserved in a tract of the Mishna as follows, " All Sacred Scriptures make the hands unclean. The Canticles and Ecclesiastes make the hands unclean. R. Jehudah saith, "Canticles make the hands unclean, but Ecclesiastes is a dispute." R. José saith, "Ecclesiastes does not make the hands unclean but the Canticles are a dispute." R. Simeon saith, "Ecclesiastes is one of those in which Beth Shammai are less strict, and Beth Hillel more rigid." R. Simeon Beth Azai said, "I have it as a tradition from the mouth of 72 elders, on the day they inducted R. Eleazer ben Azariah into the President's seat, that Canticles and Ecclesiastes both make the hands unclean." R. Akibah said, "Mercy forbid! No man in Israel ever disputed that the Canticles make the hands unclean, as the whole (history of the) world does not (offer an epoch) equal to the day on which the Canticles were given to Israel, for all the K'tubim are holy but the Canticles are Holy of Holies. The dispute referred to Ecclesiastes only." R. Jochanan ben Joshua, the son of R. Akibah's father-in-law, said, "Even as Ben Azai stated, so was the decision[2]." It has often been remarked that the energetic language of Akibah discloses the fact that serious objections had been felt to the canonicity of the book[3], and certainly a man of his fiery and impetuous nature could hardly fail to overstate anything he wished to assert. At any rate, whatever the objections were, this Synod of Jamnia finally disposed of them. "They decided in favour of the traditional claim of the Song to be inspired Holy Scripture, and this decision was

---

[1] See Graetz, *History of the Jews*, E. T., Vol. II. ch. 13.

[2] *Jadaim*, 3. 5, in Eighteen treatises of the Mishna, trans. De Sola and Raphael, London, 1845, pp. 362—3.

[3] See *e.g.* Robertson Smith, *The O. T. in the Jewish Church*, p. 174.

appealed to as authoritative some decades later when the old doubts were again raised[1]." After the days of Akibah they do not seem to have ever been raised again. The Christian Church took over from the Jewish Church a settled Canon of Old Testament Scripture.

That this was so is evident from an epistle written by Melito bishop of Sardis to his friend Onesimus (cir. 160, about 60 years after Josephus wrote)[2]. In this epistle, after remarking that his friend was desirous of having an exact statement of the Old Testament, how many in number and in what order the books were written, he goes on: "When therefore I went to the East and came as far as the place where these things were proclaimed and done, I accurately ascertained the books of the Old Testament and send them to thee here below." And his list is the same in effect as that of Josephus, with the exception of Esther which, either by accident or design (it is not here relevant to enquire which), is omitted.

The later catalogues of Origen (cir. 250)[3] and Jerome[4] are practically the same, and they make it clear that the early Christian Church accepted the Palestinian Canon of the Hebrew Scriptures in its entirety. The Song of Songs has always been included in the Christian Canon of Scripture.

15. ALLEGORICAL INTERPRETATION.

We shall not be much at a loss to discover why objections arose in the minds of pious and orthodox Jews as to the retention of Canticles in the Canon of Sacred Scripture. There was no difficulty about its antiquity. If, as has been suggested above, it had been preserved in Jerusalem with other works attributed to Solomon from the days of Hezekiah, it was far older than the days of Ezra—and it does not appear that anyone ever doubted its age. But the Canon of Scripture was supposed only to contain books of a religious character, and the Song, venerable as it was, appeared to be a secular book.

---

[1] Budde, p. IX.
[2] Eusebius, *H. E.* IV. 26. Original in Ryle, Excursus D.
[3] Eusebius, *H. E.* VI. 25. Original in Ryle, Excursus D.
[4] Prologus Galeatus. Original in Ryle, Excursus D.

Undoubtedly, objectors were silenced, and the position of the book as Holy Scripture was maintained, by the fact that it had begun to be interpreted allegorically[1]. If Josephus could call it "a hymn to God," and R. Akiba pronounce it holier than all the other K'tubim, and if the opposition to it was slightly felt and soon disappeared, it must have been because it was understood in a secondary and a religious sense. And this was undoubtedly the case. It became a principle of exegesis that "one who scans the Song of Solomon like a secular poem has no share in the world to come[2]." A few examples of this allegorising method may be given here.

The oldest example is said to be found in 2 Esdras (written sometime in the reign of Domitian and therefore about the time of the Synod of Jamnia). In this book the holy nation of Israel is compared, v. 24, to the one *lily* among all flowers; v. 26, to the one *dove* among all birds; vii. 26, to the appearing *bride*, all images taken from the Song.

Other passages from Talmudic tracts later in date, are as follows. "It is written (Cant. vii. 3, quoted): *Thy body is like a heap of wheat* refers to the Assembly of Israel, and *fenced about with lilies,* refers to the 70 elders. Another explanation of the words, *Thy body is like a heap of wheat* is that they refer to the lenient religious duties which seem to be of no consequence, *fenced about with lilies,* nevertheless when the Israelites perform them, they bring them to the world to come[3]."

"He used to say the words (Cant. i. 6, quoted) refer to the councillors of Judah who relieved themselves of the yoke of the Holy One (blessed be He), and chose a human king to reign over them. *My mother's children were angry with me* refers to Moses who slew the Egyptian. The rest of the verse refers to the Israelites who were exiled in Babylon; and the prophets, who were then among them, told them to observe the laws of offerings and tithes. They however answered, 'We were exiled because we refused to observe those laws, and you wish us to observe them now[4].'"

"(On Cant. iii. 11) *The day of the espousals* refers to the

---

[1] See Renan, p. 123; Budde, p. x; Riedel, p. 3.
[2] *Aboth R. Nathan*, Rodkinson, 1. 122. Compare note 4, p. 84, *sup.*
[3] *Aboth R. Nathan*, Rodkinson, 1. 13.
[4] *Ib.* 1. 72—4.

day on which the law was given and *the day of the joy of his heart* was that when the building of the temple was completed. May it soon be rebuilt in our days[1]!"

"(On Cant. i. 2) How are the words *Thy love is better than wine* understood? When R. Dimi came to Babylon he said, "This verse is thus understood, the Congregation of Israel said to God, 'Lord of the Universe, the words of thy friends (namely, the sages) are more excellent than even the wine of the law[2].'"

These few specimens (which might be multiplied) are enough to shew how this style of interpretation entirely disregarded the primary meaning of the poem. Any interpretation seemed admissible which tended either to instruction or edification, or which gave scope to the acuteness or ingenuity of the Rabbinical expositor. No one seemed for a moment to consider what the author had in view when he wrote any passage. "The beloved" is usually interpreted as "the Lord," "the bride" (as in 2 Esdras), "the Congregation of Israel."

The *Targum* is a complete Commentary on the Song. Though not written down until the 6th century, the materials of which it is composed are undoubtedly of much earlier date, and it embodies much of the allegorical exposition contained in the Talmud[3]. The Targum takes the Song of Songs as an allegory describing the history of the Jewish nation, beginning with the Exodus from Egypt, describing the sin of the golden Calf, the erection of the Tabernacle, the conquest of Canaan, the building of Solomon's temple, the Babylonian captivity, the deliverance through Cyrus, the building of the second Temple, the days of the Maccabees, and the dispersion of the Jews. It finally prophesies the coming of king Messiah, the resurrection of the dead, the final ingathering of Israel, and the third temple on Mount Zion. In working out these allegories the connection of the commentary with the text is very slight, often far-fetched and even capricious. The

---

[1] *Taanith*, 4. 8. Rodkinson, 8. 80.
[2] *Abodah Sarah*, quoted Ginsburg, p. 20.
[3] Ginsburg, p. 28 foll. Riedel, *Die Auslegung des H. L.* p. 8. (This valuable work contains a complete translation of the Targum with most useful notes.) The extracts in the text are taken from the translation by H. Gollancz, Lusac and Co. 1909.

interpretation is often obtained by substituting in the comment words somewhat similar but of different sense to those in the text. A few extracts will suffice to show how the allegory is worked out.

i. 5, *I am black*, &c. "When the Israelites fashioned the Calf, their faces darkened as those of the children of Ethiopia, who dwell in the tents of Kedar: when they turned in penitence, and their guilt was pardoned, the brilliant radiance of their countenance increased as that of the angels; (this occurred) when they made the curtains for the Tabernacle, and the Divine Presence once again dwelt in their midst, when Moses, their teacher, went up to Heaven, and brought about peace[1] between them and their king."

i. 6, *Look not on me*, &c. "The Assembly of Israel addresses the nations thus:—Despise me not, in that I am darker than you; (it is) because I have done according to your actions, and bowed down to the sun and moon; false prophets have been the cause of it, in order to draw down upon me the fury of the anger of the Lord: they taught me to worship your idols, and to walk according to your laws, whilst the Sovereign of the Universe, my own God, I did not serve, I did not go after his laws, nor did I keep His statutes nor His law."

i. 7, *Tell me*, &c. "When the time arrived for Moses the prophet to depart from this world, he said before the Lord:— It is revealed to me that this people will sin, and be carried into captivity. Inform me, I pray thee, how they will sustain themselves, and how they will live among the nations, whose decrees are as violent as the heat, yea as the heat of the noonday sun in the summer solstice; inform me whether they shall be carried away among the flocks of the children of Esau and Ishmael who associate with Thy service their idol worship."

iv. 1, *Behold thou art fair*, &c. "Now on that day king Solomon sacrificed on the altar a thousand burnt offerings, and his offering was accepted with favour by the Lord, whereupon the Bath Kol proceeded from Heaven and said:—How comely art thou, O Assembly of Israel, and how comely are those leaders of the Assembly, and those wise men, sitting in the Sanhedrin, who for ever enlighten the people of Israel,

---

[1] שלמה = King of Peace.

resembling young pigeons, and even the rest of the children of thy Assembly, the people of the land, they are righteous as the sons of Jacob, who gathered stones and made a heap in the mountain of Gilead!"

iv. 3, *Thy lips*, &c. "And the lips of the High Priest uttered prayers on the Atonement-Day before the Lord, and his words had the effect of turning away the sins of Israel, which, appearing as the scarlet thread, were changed and became white as pure wool. As for the king at the head of it all, he was as full of religious practice as the pomegranate, as well as the overseers and chiefs that stood in close relation to the king, who were righteous, and in whom there was no guile whatsoever."

vi. 8, *There are threescore queens*, &c. "Then there arose the Greeks, and gathered together sixty kings from the children of Esau, clothed in mail, riding upon horses, and horsemen, and eighty dukes of the children of Ishmael, riding upon elephants, besides those of other peoples and tongues without number, and they appointed king Alexander as the chief over them, and came to wage war against Jerusalem."

vi. 9, *My dove*, &c. "Now at that time the Assembly of Israel, resembling a perfect dove, was serving her Sovereign Lord with one heart, and cleaving to the law, busy with the practice of its ordinances with a perfect heart, and their merit was as clear as on the day of the Exodus from Egypt. On this account, when the Hasmoneans with Mattathias and all the people of Israel came forth and engaged in battle with them, the Eternal delivered the enemy into their hands, and as the inhabitants of the districts saw this, they blessed them, and the kings of the land and the rulers praised them."

These few extracts are enough to shew the edifice of allegorical comment which grew up around the Song, and how little these parables had to do with the text they were supposed to illustrate. Of the primary meaning of that text, of what the author meant when he wrote it, they seem to have had no idea; its words merely formed the basis on which they might erect their historic or prophetic fancies. It is a wonderful phenomenon. While their nation was in the depth of degradation and ruin, and while for centuries persecution and infamy were the daily portion of the Jew, these earnest acute Rabbis, in their schools at Tiberias and Babylon, were building up this fabric of mystical exposition, dwelling on the glorious past of their oppressed race and foretelling its splendid future. These visions, which were to bring hope and comfort to many a Jew as he languished in the Ghetto of some proud city, or pored over Rabbinical tomes in the Beth-ham-Midrash of some lonely hamlet, had really nothing to do with the text they were supposed to illustrate. The old Ephraimite poem of youth and spring and triumphant love was buried and lost amidst this *mélange* of history and legend and vision, which R. Akiba and his successors so incongruously heaped upon it by way of "explaining" it. Certainly the author never thought as he described his sunburnt heroine, that he was referring to the sin of Israel with the golden calf, or that his allusion to Solomon's harem was really a prophecy of the Syro-Greek armies marching against the Maccabees!

When the Christian Church took over from the Synagogue the Canon of Old Testament Scripture, the mystical interpretation of the Song came with its Text. This was indeed inevitable, no other principle of explanation was, at that time, admissible, nor, until recent times, has any other method of interpretation prevailed[1]. The allegorical treatment appears in a complete form in the Homilies and Commentary of *Origen* (185—254), where it may best be studied[2]. These works derive their special value from several reasons. The author was not only well versed in Hebrew, but was a man of deep religious feeling, with an immense knowledge of Scripture, and an earnest desire to bring out its fullest meaning for the instruction of the Church. His work enjoyed the highest estimation both in his own days and with later generations, as may be seen from the testimony of Jerome, who declared that in his Commentaries generally Origen excelled all others, but in commenting on the Song he excelled himself (*vicit se*). And the work of Origen is also of great importance because he was the founder of the recognised interpretation of the Song in the Christian Church. "He marked in it once for all the main lines of allegorical interpretation

---

[1] See, *e.g.*, Kingsbury in the *Speaker's Comm.* (1873), IV. 674.

[2] The two Homilies (trans. by Jerome) and the four books of Commentaries (to c. ii. 15, trans. by Rufinus) are in *Orig. Opp.* ed. Delarue, Paris, 1740, III. 12—110. The writer has derived much help from the admirable dissertation of Riedel, *op. cit.* pp. 52—66.

which later commentators followed[1]" and may thus, in a general way, represent for us the whole Christian tradition. It has been already observed[2] that Origen recognised that the Song was *dramatic* and that he distinguished four *persons*; or rather two persons and two chorus-groups. But on the distribution of the speeches between these various characters he is very uncertain[3], and it is very difficult to see that he had any grasp of the story or argument of the poem. In every section of his exposition he recognizes that there is a primary historical sense, and endeavours to bring it out, and in one place (on ii. 8, 14) he recapitulates the sense of several verses. But all is vague, shadowy, and unconvincing; he seems to have little sense of the fact that there is a real living story in the poem, it rather seems to him a series of dialogues, which are from their nature suited to be mystically interpreted. And he certainly was much impeded in obtaining the true sense of the text by the fact that he constantly used the LXX. text (which he believed to be inspired) even although he must have known that it differed (and almost invariably for the worse) from the Hebrew[4]. Such versions as *Traxerunt* &c., i. 4, *Aequitas* dilexit &c., *ib.*, *Pelles Salamonis*, i. 5, *Similitudines* auri faciemus tibi (non enim habemus aurum), i. 10, *Introducite me...ordinate in me* caritatem, ii. 4, Adjuravi vos, filiae Jerus. in *virtutibus* et in *viribus* agri, ii. 7, and the monstrous *dealbata*, viii. 5, might and did lend themselves to beautiful spiritual exposition, but could only lead the expositor away from the primary meaning of his Hebrew original.

In the allegorical scheme of Origen, the bridegroom, Solomon, the king of Peace, is naturally *Christ*[5]. The young

---

[1] Westcott, *Dict. Chris. Biog.* s.v. *Origines*, IV. 109.

[2] Sec. 5, *sup.*

[3] He wrote in his youth a little treatise Περὶ τοῦ ἰδιώματος τῶν προσώπων τῆς θείας γραφῆς, of which only a fragment is preserved, *Op.* III. p. 11 A.

[4] "Tamen nos LXX interpretum scripta *per omnia* custodimus," III. 41 D. See Westcott in the article *sup. cit.* IV. 132.

[5] Christum sponsum intellige. 12 B.

Sponsus qui est sermo Dei. 26 A.

In plurimis Sal. X^m typum ferre, vel secundum quod pacificus dicitur; vel secundum hoc quod regina austri venit a finibus terrae audire sapientiam Sal^i non puto dubitandum. Hic ergo et secundum quod filius David dicitur....Et rursus verus Ecclesiastes ipse est. 35 A.

men who surround Him, his companions, are sometimes His Angels, sometimes the Prophets and Patriarchs, who revealed the Logos, sometimes the Teachers of the Church. They are variously understood according to the contents of the verse which is being explained. And, as we have seen already, the bridegroom and the shepherd are the same[1].

As regards the *Bride* a distinction has been noted between the Homilies and the Commentaries. In the former the Bride is the Church, the holy and undefiled one, the sister of the Synagogue[2]. But in the Commentaries the Bride is first the Church and secondly the individual faithful Soul[3], and on i. 5 the Gentile Church[4]. And so on each verse there is first an explanation of the historical or primary sense, then an allegorical exposition applying the passage to the Church, and then a third, applying it to the Soul in union with the Word. It has been acutely remarked[5] that as the work proceeds the third meaning grows more and more interesting and precious to the author.

The maidens who accompany the Bride, are the incomplete and unripe Christian souls—the catechumens—while the daughters of Jerusalem, who form a different group, represent the Jews who have not believed. The following extracts will afford a fair idea of Origen's methods of exposition.

On i. 5. (1) Primary interpretation.

"Here again is introduced the person of the bride speaking, but speaking not to those maidens who are accustomed to run with her, but to the daughters of Jerusalem, to whom, as if to those who have disparaged her on account of her ugliness, she seems to reply and say, 'Dusky indeed I am, or black as regards colour, daughters of Jerusalem, but beautiful if anyone will have regard to the inner features of the members. For,' says she, 'the tabernacles of Kedar, a mighty race, are black, and that race of Kedar is, being interpreted, blackness or obscurity.

---

[1] Quia sponsus hic etiam pastor fit. 54 B.

[2] Ecclesiam sponsam sine macula et ruga (intellige). 12 B.

[3] Sponsa, animam vel ecclesiam. 26 A.

Spiritualis (expositio)...vel de ecclesia ad X^m sub sponsae vel sponsi titulo, vel de animae cum Verbo Dei conjunctione dirigitur. 36 E.

[4] Haec sponsa quae loquitur ecclesiae personam tenet ex gentibus congregatae. 46 B.

[5] Riedel, p. 60.

But Solomon's tents (pelles) are also black, yet, because the king is so glorious in all things, the blackness of his tents does not seem unbecoming. Do not then, oh daughters of Jerusalem, upbraid me for the defect of colour, since beauty, whether natural or gained by exercise, is not wanting to my body.' This is what the historical drama contains, and the idea of the story intended by it."

(2) Mysticus ordo. (a) The Church, (b) The Soul.

" This bride who speaks represents the part of the Church collected from the nations. But the daughters of Jerusalem to whom she addresses herself, they are souls who indeed are called most dear because of the election of the fathers, but enemies for the Gospel's sake. Such are the daughters of Jerusalem the earthly city, who when they see a Church out of the nations although base-born in this respect that she cannot claim the noble birth of Abraham, Isaac and Jacob, yet forgetting her own people and her father's house until she come to Christ, they scorn her and blacken her because she is of lowly origin. So when the bride feels that the daughters of the older people blame her, and that for this cause she is called black, as if she had not the brightness of the learning of the fathers, she says in reply to these things, " I am indeed black, oh daughters of Jerusalem, because I do not descend from the stock of honourable men, nor did I receive the light of Moses' law, yet I have about me a beauty of my own. For that first thing there is in me which was made in me according to the image of God, and now, coming to the Word of God, I have received my beauty. For although on account of darkness of colour you may liken me to the tabernacles of Kedar and the tents of Solomon, yet Kedar too is a descendant of Ishmael. For he was born of Ishmael in a subordinate rank, since Ishmael had no share in the Divine blessing. But you liken me also to Solomon's tents which are none other than the coverings of the Tabernacle of God, and yet I marvel, oh daughters of Jerusalem, that you wish to blame the blackness of my colour."

He then discusses at great length the various *dark persons* mentioned in Scripture—the Ethiopian wife of Moses (Num. xii.), the Queen of Sheba (1 Kings x.) and Ebed-melech, the Ethiopian, who drew Jeremiah out of the pit (Jer. xxxviii.) and allegorises in various ways their stories, and then remarks:

"This dark or black and comely one has therefore many evidences on which she may freely act, and say with confidence to the daughters of Jerusalem, *I am black but comely*, &c."

Then he proceeds to discuss Solomon's tents in connection with the Jewish Tabernacle and concludes, "But in that it appears to be one person who speaks and she compares herself to many, either to tabernacles of Kedar in blackness or to tents of Solomon, it is to be taken in this way—because one person indeed appears, yet there are innumerable churches scattered over the world and immense congregations and multitudes of people—just as the Kingdom of Heaven is said to be one, and yet there are said to be in it many mansions in the Father's house. But it may also be said of *every soul* which after much sinning turns to repentance that, although it may be black through sins, it is beautiful on account of repentance and fruits of repentance. Finally also of this very one who now says, *I am black but comely*, because she has not remained to the end in blackness the daughters of Jerusalem afterwards say of this very one, *Who is this who comes up all white[1] leaning upon her brother[2]?*"

The Commentaries of Origen may not give much help to an editor in dealing with difficult problems relating to the primary meaning of the Canticles, but in themselves they are extremely interesting and inspired by deep religious emotion. After reading them it is not difficult to understand the attraction which this poem has always had for Christian saints and mystics. It is not so much the old Ephraimite poem as the powerful allegory which Origen has made out of it which caused it to be, for many centuries, so precious to the Christian Church.

The *Targum* and *Origen* have been selected as typical examples of Jewish and Christian methods of interpreting the Song as an allegory. Little would be gained by examining the vagaries and extravagances which have been perpetrated by other expositors down to comparatively late times. The reader will probably be satisfied with the following summary of them. "This book is made to describe the most contradictory things. It contains the wanderings of the Jews, how they will ultimately 'fill their stomachs with the flesh of the Leviathan,

---

[1] dealbata viii. 5 = λελευκανθισμένη. See Excursus I.
[2] III. 45 foll.

and the best of wines preserved in grapes,' and is the sanctum sanctorum of all Christian mysteries. It is denounced as a love song, and extolled as declaring the incarnation of Christ; it speaks of the meridian church in Africa, and of the betrayal of the Saviour; it contains a treatise upon the doctrine of free grace against Pelagianism, and an Aristotelian disquisition upon the functions of the active and passive mind; it is an apocalyptic vision, a duplicate of the Revelations of Saint John, and records the scholastic mysticisms of the middle ages; it denounces Arianism, and describes the glories of the Virgin Mary; it 'treats of man's reconciliation unto God and peace by Jesus Christ with joy in the Holy Ghost,' and teaches lewdness and corrupts morals; it records the conversation of Solomon and Wisdom, and describes the tomb of Christ in Egyptian hieroglyphics; it celebrates the nuptials of Solomon, and gives us a compendium of ecclesiastical history to the second advent of Christ; it records the restoration of a Jewish constitution by Zerubbabel, Ezra and Nehemiah, and the mysteries of marriage; it advocates monogamy and encourages polygamy; it assists devotion and excites carnal passions[1]."

It has been shewn above how the idea arose that the Song ought to be allegorically interpreted; but the mass of incongruities just quoted must tend to shew how essentially unsatisfactory this method of explanation must be. It is perhaps rather a question of theology whether any allegorical interpretation of the Song or any other Old Testament Scripture is legitimate, and it will not be discussed here. It is enough to state as a literary fact that the Song does not disclose any intention on the part of its author that it should be understood or interpreted as an allegory.

Indeed, its primary meaning, properly understood, abundantly vindicates its inclusion in the Sacred Canon. Its powerful ethical purpose will always justify its retention there. It is not out of date nor outworn, nor is it to be thought that it ever will be. Fidelity in pure and chaste love will always be admirable and praiseworthy; polygamy and wantonness will always be things to protest against. The noble declaration that love ought to be spontaneous, not bought, not forced, not

---

[1] Ginsburg, pp. 101—2.

artificially excited, is as valid now as it was in the period of Solomon. Such truths can never be obsolete, they touch some of the deepest and most permanent elements in human nature. Just as David's great elegy on the death of Saul and Jonathan (2 Sam. i. 19), purely secular in tone though it be, could not be spared from the Sacred Canon, neither could the Song. Holy Scripture would be less perfect than it is, its appeal to the human heart would lack something, did it not include poems which, though not religious, yet touch the profoundest and most sacred of human emotions, *Friendship* and *Love*.

THE SONG OF SONGS[1]

CANTO I. c. I.—II. 7

(a) I. 2—8

COURT LADIES

2 Oh that he would kiss me with kisses of his mouth
  For thy caresses are better than wine.
3 For perfume thine unguents are good,
  An unguent poured forth is thy name[2],
  Therefore maidens love thee.

SHULAMITE

4 Draw me after thee, oh let us run away[3],
  The king has brought me into his apartments.

LADIES

We will exult and rejoice in thee,
We will praise thy caresses more than wine,
Ah! they are in the right who love thee.

SHULAMITE

5 I am black yet comely, oh ye daughters of Jerusalem,
  As tents of Kedar, as pavilions of Solomon.

---

[1] In a few places the Heb. text has been amended from the LXX. All these places are discussed in Excursus I.

[2] Against the ordinary accents, but there is authority for this pointing Wickes, *Prose Accents*, p. 141.

[3] This is also against the accents, but there is authority. Baer, Quinque vol. p. 45; and the Targum must have read this.

6 Do not gaze upon me, because I am swarthy,
   Because the sun hath glared upon me[1].
   My mother's sons were angry with me,
   They appointed me keeper of the vineyards,
   My own vineyard I have not kept.
7 Tell me, oh thou whom my soul loveth,
   Where thou feedest (thy flock),
   Where thou makest it lie down at noon,
   Why should I be like one wandering[2] among the flocks
       of thy companions?

LADIES

8 If thou dost not know, oh thou fairest among women,
   Go thy way forth at the heels of the flock,
   And feed thy kids beside the shepherds' tents.

(b) I. 9—II. 7

SOLOMON

9   To my mare in Pharaoh's chariots,
    I liken thee, oh my friend.
10 Thy cheeks are comely with chains,
    Thy neck with necklaces.
11 We will make thee chains of gold,
    With studs of silver.

---

[1] שְׁזָפַתְנִי. This word is used Job xx. 9, xxviii. 7 in the sense of "a fixed gaze," in the latter passage of a bird of prey. So LXX. and S¹ παρέβλεψε; Sym. παρενέβλεψε; Gr.-Ven. κατεῖδε; Brown, *Lex.* "looked"; Kingsbury, "glared"; Siegf. "ausgestrahlt." Another proposed meaning connects the word with שׂרף, Gen. xli. 23, in the sense of "burned," "scorched." Aq. συνέκαυσε, Theod. περιέφρυξε. So Buhl, *Lex.*: Del., Ew., Hitz., Renan, Bruston. A third view is that of the Vul. *decoloravit* (so Pesh.) in the sense "blackened or browned," so Rothst., Ginsb., Oettli. Of these three possible meanings the first is adopted here (1) because it has definite Old Test. authority and yields an excellent sense, (2) because it is more poetical, "The sun glared at me like a fierce bird of prey."

[2] For עֹטְיָה, which is very unsuitable and gives a very poor sense, read תֹעִיָה = טֹעִיָה (Gen. xxxvii. 15; Ex. xxiii. 4; Prov. xxi. 16) with Sym. ῥεμβο-μένη, Pesh. To'ito, Vulg. *vagari incipiam*, Gr.-Ven. ἐκνεύουσα, Ges. K. 75, Anm. 1, v. Boetticher, L. G. 470, n. 1.

SHULAMITE

12 So long as the king was at his banquet[1],
My spikenard gave forth its perfume.
13 A bag of myrrh is my beloved to me,
Which lodgeth in my bosom.
14 A cluster of henna flowers is my beloved to me,
In the vineyards of En-gedi.

SOLOMON

15 Behold thou art fair, my friend,
Behold thou art fair—thine eyes are doves.

SHULAMITE

16 Behold thou art fair, my beloved, and pleasant,
Yea, our couch is green.
17 The beams of our houses are cedars,
Our rafters, cypresses.
II 1. I am a narcissus[2] of Sharon,
A lily of the valleys.

SOLOMON

2 Like a lily among thorns,
So is my friend among the daughters.

SHULAMITE

3 Like an apple-tree among the trees of the wood,
So is my beloved among the sons.
I sat down under his shade with great delight,
And his fruit was sweet to my palate.
4 He brought me to the house of wine,
And his banner over me was love.

---

[1] מֵסַב is so rendered by all the versions. See the verb in 1 Sam. xvi. 11.

[2] Opinions have differed as to what flower is meant by חֲבַצֶּלֶת here and Is. xxxv. 1; LXX. ἄνθος; Vulg. *flos*; Aq. καλύκωσις, rosebud; Gr.-Ven. ῥόδον; Pesh. *Shushanath*, in both halves of the verse, but *Chamzaljotho*, autumn crocus, in Is., which is adopted here by many Comm.; Targum נַרְקִים רַטִיב, which seems most suitable. The white narcissus dotting a green expanse is the very image of modesty and beauty.

5 Support me with grape cakes[1],
  Refresh me with apples,
  For I am sick with love.
6 Oh! that his left hand were under my head,
  And that his right hand did embrace me.
7 I adjure you, daughters of Jerusalem, by the gazelles,
  Or by the hinds of the field,
  That ye stir not up and awaken not Love,
  Until it please.

CANTO II. c. II. 8—III. 5

(a) II. 8—17

SHULAMITE

8 Hark! my beloved! Behold there he cometh,
  Leaping upon the mountains,
  Skipping upon the hills.
9 My beloved is like a gazelle or a young hart.
  Behold there he is, standing behind our wall,
  Gazing through the windows,
  Glancing through the lattices.
10 My beloved speaks—he speaks to me[2]!
  "Rise up, my friend, my fair one, and come away.
11 For lo the winter is past,
  The rain is over, is gone[3].
12 The flowers appear in the land,
  The time of singing is come[4],
  And the voice of the turtle is heard in our land.

---

[1] See 2 Sam. vi. 19; 1 Chron. xvi. 3; Is. xvi. 7 (with Cheyne's note); Hosea iii. 1 (adds עֲנָבִים).

[2] Oettli proposes to read עֹנֶה and אֹמֵר to agree with the other participles, but this is not necessary. The perfects here have a present sense. See Driver, *Tenses*, sec. 10; *Ges. K.* 106. 2 i(b).

[3] Some MSS. read וְהָלַךְ but are not followed by the LXX. See Baer, p. 46.

[4] זָמִיר. All the versions and the Targum as well as many editors translate this word "pruning" of the vine, and the form of the word is in favour of this (comp. קָצִיר, &c.; *Ges. K.* 84 a, l). Still this is rather tame in so poetic a passage; the time for pruning is past when the vines are in bloom. It is better to take this as the same word as זָמִיר, Is. xxv. 5 (often in plur., 2 Sam. xxiii. 1; Ps. xcv. 2, &c.), meaning "song" not of birds but of men. Possibly the vowelling may indicate a provincial variation.

13 The fig-tree ripeneth her green figs,
   And the vines are in bloom, they diffuse fragrance.
   Rise up, my friend my fair one, and come away[1].
14 Oh! my dove in the clefts of the rock,
   In the hidden places of the precipices,
   Let me see thy countenance,
   Let me hear thy voice,
   For sweet is thy voice and thy countenance is comely."
15 "Catch us the foxes, the little foxes,
   Destroyers of vineyards,
   For our vineyards are in bloom."
16 My beloved is mine, and I am his,
   He who feeds (his flock) among the lilies.
17 Until the day breathes forth, and the shadows flee away,
   Turn away[2], my beloved.
   Be like a gazelle or a young hart,
   Upon craggy mountains[3].

(b) III. 1—5

1 On my bed by night,
  I sought him whom my soul loveth,
  I sought him but I found him not.
2[4] "Ah, let me arise and go about in the city,
  In the streets, and in the broad places,
  Let me seek him whom my soul loveth,"
  I sought him but I found him not.
3 The watchmen that go about in the city found me.
  "Have ye seen him whom my soul loveth?"
4 Scarcely had I passed from them,
  When I found him whom my soul loveth,

---

[1] Reading the K'ri לָךְ (for לְכִי) as v. 10.

[2] סֹב here is the equivalent of בְּרַח, viii. 14. Rightly LXX. ἀπόστρεψον, not Vulg. *revertere.*

[3] בֶּתֶר here might be a proper name, *Bithron,* 2 Sam. ii. 9, but on the analogy of viii. 14 is more likely an epithet of some kind. The reading of the LXX. κοιλωμάτων gives an excellent sense, "mountains of ravines," steep craggy mountains, and gazelles are often seen upon such mountains.

[4] Here אָמַרְתִּי (vii. 9) should be supplied in thought as with the same word אָקוּמָה, Job xix. 18. See 2 Sam. xxii. 38; Hab. ii. 1; Driver, *Tenses,* sec. 54.

I held him and I did not let him go[1],
Until I brought him to my mother's house,
And to the chamber of her that conceived me.

5 I adjure you, daughters of Jerusalem, by the gazelles,
Or by the hinds of the field,
That ye stir not up and awaken not Love
Until it please.

CANTO III. c. III. 6—V. 8.

(a) III. 6—11

THE POET

6 What[2] is this coming up from the country,
Like pillars of smoke;
Perfumed with myrrh and frankincense,
With all aromatic powders of the merchant?

7 Behold, it is Solomon's litter,
Sixty heroes around it,
Of the heroes of Israel;

8 Every one of them armed with a sword,
Expert in war;
Each with his sword on his thigh,
Because of terror at night.

9 [King Solomon made himself a palanquin
Of the wood of Lebanon;

10 Its pillars he made of silver,
Its back of gold,
Its seat of purple,
Its interior inlaid in lovely fashion[3]
By the daughters of Jerusalem[4].]

---

[1] So most editors, who agree that the *vav* is consec.; see Jer. xliv. 22; Job xxiii. 11; Driver, *Tenses*, sec. 85. Ewald took the verb as a future. LXX. B and others ἀφῆκα, A ἀφήσω, Vulg. *dimittam*.

[2] It would seem that מִי may be used of things as well as of persons, when the idea of persons underlies the things (Gen. xxxiii. 8; Judges xiii. 17; Micah i. 8; *Ges. K.* 37. 1 a, 136 c, 137 a). זֹאת is fem. to agree with מִטָּתוֹ, v. 7. Budde proposes to read מַה־זֹּאת.

[3] Taking אַהֲבָה adverbially (Hos. xiv. 4; Gins. *Com.*; *Ges. K.* 118. 5. 9) and מִן as used of the author or instrument (Is. xxii. 3, xxviii. 7). See some remarks on this passage in Excursus II.

[4] These verses (9, 10) may perhaps be a later gloss. See Excursus II.

11 Go forth and gaze, daughters of Zion, on King Solomon,
In the crown wherewith his mother crowned him
On his marriage day,
And on the day of the gladness of his heart.

(b) IV. 1—7

SOLOMON

1 Behold thou art fair, my friend, behold thou art fair,
Thine eyes are doves, behind thy veil;
Thy hair is like a flock of goats,
That come down[1] from Gilead.

2 Thy teeth are like a flock of shorn sheep,
Which have come up from the washing;
Whereof every one hath twins,
And none is barren among them.

3 Thy lips are like a thread of scarlet,
And thy mouth[2] is comely;
Thy temples are like a piece of a pomegranate,
Behind thy veil.

4 Thy neck is like the Tower of David,
Built for an arsenal[3];
A thousand bucklers are hung upon it,
All the shields of the heroes.

---

[1] גָּלְשׁוּ. This variously interpreted word seems to mean "to roll down like a wave." See the late Jewish-Aramaic noun גְּלְשָׁא, "when a woman has much hair she makes it into waves (גָּלְשִׁין)." Levy, neu-heb. Wörterbuch, s.v.

[2] Reading the K'ri without the yod, Baer, 48. The word does not mean "speech" (LXX. λαλιά, Gr.-Ven. διάλογός, Vulg. eloquium) but the "organ of speech," to agree with the other half of the sentence.

[3] This seems the best translation of the difficult word תַּלְפִּיּוֹת. There is a root לְפִי, לְפָה or לוּף meaning "to put or lay together" (Levy, neu-heb. Wörterbuch; see Rothstein, das H. L. 1893, p. 60) from which this word is probably derived. It would then mean "the place of bringing together," and the other half verse would explain what is brought together, i.e. "arms." So Renan, "pour servir d'arsénal"; Bruston, "pour déposer des armes." The ingenious conjecture of Dalman (in Kittel's Bib. Heb.), תְּלִיּוֹת (Gen. xxvii. 3), would be mere tautology in view of the word תְּלִי in the next line, and the sense of the passage requires a more general expression. As to the LXX. and other Gk. versions see Excursus I end.

5   Thy two breasts are like twin fawns of the gazelle,
    Which feed among the lilies.—
6   Until the day breathes forth, and the shadows flee away,
    I will get me to the mount of myrrh,
    And to the hill of frankincense.
7   Thou art all fair my friend,
    And there is no blemish in thee!

(c) IV. 8—V. 1

THE BELOVED

8   With me from Lebanon, oh betrothed,
    With me from Lebanon thou shalt come;
    Thou shalt journey[1] from the top of Amana,
    From the top of Senir[2] and Hermon,
    From dens of lions,
    From mountains of panthers.
9   Thou dost give me courage[3], my sister betrothed,
    Thou dost give me courage with one look from thine eyes[4],
    With one link of thy necklace.
10 How much fairer are thy caresses, my sister betrothed,
    How much fairer are thy caresses than wine,
    And the scent of thine unguents than all perfumes.
11 Honey do thy lips distil, oh betrothed,
    Honey and milk are under thy tongue,
    And the smell of thy garments is like the smell of Lebanon.
12 A garden locked is my sister betrothed,
    A garden locked, a fountain sealed.
13 Thy plants are a garden of pomegranates,
    With precious fruits,
    Henna flowers with spikenards.

---

[1] This sense of תָּשׁוּרִי is proved by Is. lvii. 9 and the versions. "So wird durch das 'Hinweggehen vom Lib.' das 'Herabschauen vom Amana' einfach ausgeschlossen."—Hitzig, *Com.*

[2] "שְׂנִיר cum Sin apud omnes certos testes," Baer, p. 48.

[3] לְבַּבְתְּנִי. So Sym. ἐθάρσυνας and the Syr.; see the Pesh. 1 Thess. v. 14. See the Niph. Job xi. 12 (Volck: Cook in *Speaker's Com.*).

[4] The K'tib בְּאַחַד is to be preferred to the K'ri. Not "with one of thine eyes" but "with one (look) from thine eyes." See Oettli, *Com.*

14 Spikenard with saffron, calamus and cinnamon,
 With all trees of frankincense;
 Myrrh and aloes with all chief spices.
15 A garden fountain, a well of living waters,
 And[1] streams from Lebanon.

SHULAMITE

16 Awake! thou North wind, and come, thou South wind,
 Blow upon my garden, that the spices thereof may flow out,
 Let my beloved come to his garden,
 And eat his precious fruits!

THE BELOVED

V 1 I come to my garden, my sister betrothed[2],
 I gather my myrrh with my spice,
 I eat my honeycomb with my honey[3],
 I drink my wine with my milk!

THE POET

Eat, oh friends, drink and be drunk with caresses[4].

(d) V. 2—8

SHULAMITE

2 I was asleep, but my heart was awake;
 Hark! my beloved, knocking at the door,
 "Open to me, my sister, my friend, my dove, my perfect
  one,
 For my head is filled with dew,
 My locks with drops of the night."

---

[1] The *vav* should be read, Baer, p. 48, with LXX. against Vulg. and Pesh.

[2] The preterites in this verse are the so-called *Perff. confidentiæ*, "to indicate actions the accomplishment of which lies indeed in the future, but is regarded as dependent upon such an unalterable determination of the will, that it may be spoken of as having actually taken place." Driver, *Tenses*, sec. 13; *Ges. K.* 106. 3 n.

[3] נֹפֶת, Honigseim; דְּבַשׁ, Dattelhonig. Graetz, *Com.*

[4] So the Gr.-Ven. μεθύσθητε ἔρωσιν. There seems no reason why דּוֹדִים should have a different meaning here than in every other place in the Song.

3 "I have put off my garment, how shall I put it on,
　 I have washed my feet, how shall I defile them?"
4 My beloved put his hand through the hole—
　 How my heart yearned for him[1]!
5 I rose to open to my beloved,
　 And my hands dropped myrrh,
　 And my fingers running myrrh,
　 Upon the wards of the lock.
6 I opened to my beloved,
　 But my beloved had turned away, had gone.
　 My soul departed when he went away[2],
　 I sought him, but I found him not,
　 I called him, but he answered me not.
7 The watchmen that go about in the city found me,
　 They smote me, they wounded me,
　 They took my veiling garment from off me,
　 Those watchmen of the walls!
8 I adjure you, daughters of Jerusalem,
　 If you should find my beloved,
　 What[3] will you tell him?
　 That I am sick with love!

CANTO IV. c. V. 9—VIII. 4

(a) V. 9—VI. 3

COURT LADIES

9 What is thy beloved more than another beloved,
　 Oh thou fairest among women?
　 What is thy beloved more than another beloved,
　 That thou didst so adjure us?

---

[1] עָלָיו is the better reading, though many Heb. mss. have עָלַי, Baer, 49.
See Hitzig, *Com.*

[2] If the reading בְּדַבְּרוֹ is to be retained the line is out of its place. The
reading בְּבָרְחוֹ gives a very appropriate sense, see Ewald, Hitzig and Oettli,
Coms., and is to be preferred.

[3] It is suggested, *Ges. K.* 137 b, note, that this phrase should be translated
as an imper., *Sagt ihm doch!* But it is surely question and answer. See the
Comm. and notice the accent, Zaqeph.

SHULAMITE

10 My beloved is white and ruddy,
Conspicuous among ten thousand[1].
11 His head is the finest gold,
His locks—waving, black as a raven.
12 His eyes—like doves over streams of water—,
Bathing in milk,
Sitting on fulness.
13 His cheeks like beds of spices, bringing forth sweet herbs,
His lips—lilies, dropping liquid myrrh,
14 His hands—golden cylinders, set with chrysolite,
His body—an art work of ivory—encrusted with sapphires,
15 His legs—white marble pillars, set on golden bases,
His appearance like Lebanon,
Choice as the cedars.
16 His mouth is all sweetness[2],
Yea—he is altogether delightful[2]!
This is my beloved and this is my friend,
Oh daughters of Jerusalem.

LADIES

VI 1 Where went thy beloved,
Oh thou fairest among women,
Where did thy beloved turn aside,
That we may seek him with thee?

SHULAMITE

2 My beloved went down to his garden,
To the beds of spices;
To feed (his flock) among the gardens,
And to gather lilies.

---

[1] רָגוּל. The best rendering is that of the Gr.-Ven. σεσημαιωμένος, which is nearer the Heb. than LXX. ἐκλελοχισμένος, Aq. ἐκλελεγμένος, Sym. ἐπίλεκτος, Vulg. electus, or the Syro-Hex. Fried. Delitzsch (Heb. lang. in the light of Assyr. research, Lond. 1883, p. 40) explains from the Assyrian, "Looked up to among ten thousand," but the phrase means, "Conspicuous (as a standard-bearer)."

[2] The plural form of these predicates adds emphasis to them. See Ges. K. 141. 2 c; Ps. cx. 3; Pr. viii. 30; Dan. ix. 23; Driver, Tenses, sec. 189. 2.

3 I am my beloved's and my beloved is mine,
He who feeds (his flock) among the lilies.

(b) VI. 4—VII. 1

SOLOMON

4 Thou art fair, my friend, as Tirzah,
Comely as Jerusalem—
Awe-inspiring as bannered hosts.

5 Turn away thine eyes from me,
For they terrify me—
Thy hair is like a flock of goats,
That come down from Gilead;

6 Thy teeth are like a flock of mother sheep,
Which have come up from the washing;
Whereof every one hath twins,
And none is barren among them.

7 Thy temples are like a piece of a pomegranate,
Behind thy veil.

8 There are sixty queens,
And eighty concubines,
And girls—innumerable.

9 One is she, my dove, my perfect one,
She is the only one of her mother[1],
The pure one of her who bore her[1].
The daughters saw her and called her happy,
The queens and the concubines, and they praised her.

10 "Who is this, who looks forth as the dawn,
Fair as the moon, pure as the sun,
Awe-inspiring as bannered hosts?"

SHULAMITE

11 To the nut garden I had gone down,
To look on the young shoots of the brook,
To see whether the vine had budded,
Whether the pomegranates were in flower.

---

[1] אַחַת, not "unique" as Ezek. vii. 5, but "one." בָּרָה, not as LXX. ἐκλεκτή, Vulg. electa, but rather "pure." Sym. καθάρα. "She is *one* compared with the many women, *pure* as opposed to them," Graetz.

12 Or ever I was aware,
    My desire had brought me,
    To the chariots of a prince's retinue[1].
VII 1 "Come back, come back, oh Shulamite,
    Come back, come back, that we may look on thee."
    "What would you look at in the Shulamite?"
    "As it were, the dance of Mahanaim[2]!"

(c) VII. 2—11

A COURT LADY

2 How fair are thy steps in the shoes, oh prince's daughter!
    The joints of thy thighs are like jewels;
    The work of an artist's hands.
3 Thy navel is a bowl, round as the moon[3],
    May it not want mixed wine!
    Thy body, a heap of wheat,
    Set about with lilies.
4 Thy two breasts are like twin fawns of the gazelle;
    Thy neck—like the ivory tower;
    Thine eyes—pools in Heshbon,
    By the gate of the populous city[4];

---

[1] The best rendering of this much debated passage seems to be the old one of Gesenius (*Thes.* 1042), *inter currus comitatus principis.* The Masora expressly states (though some oriental MSS. differ) that עַמִּי־נָדִיב are two words, Baer, 49, The yod in עַמִּי seems to be *litera compaginis* and a mark of the construct state. See *Ges. K.* 90. 3 k, l. The word עַם may be used to denote "companions," "attendants." See Eccl. iv. 16 and Ginsburg's *Com.* So Renan, Bruston, Haupt, *Biblische Liebeslieder*, Anm. 1. 21.

[2] Budde thinks that הַמַּחֲנָיִם cannot be the name of the town Mahanaim, as this never has the article. But the word here is in the genitive (which is not the case in the other instances, Gen. xxxii. 3; Jos. xiii. 26, 30, xxi. 39; 2 Sam. ii. 8, 12, 29, xvii. 24, 27; 1 Kgs. ii. 8, iv. 14, where it is named) and the article is used to determine the *nomen regens.* See *Ges. K.* 127 a, b; Cant. iii. 9, vii. 5; Del. *Com.*, p. 35 note. The phrase means "The (celebrated) dance of Mahanaim." In any case the point is not conclusive. In Jerem. *the same place* is called רָמָה (31. 14) and הָרָמָה (40. 1).

[3] See the Gr. Ven. ῥάντιστρον Ἑκάτης and v. Gebhardt's note. See also Targ. סִיהֲרָא here and vi. 10.

[4] בַּת־רַבִּים might be a proper name, but probably it is better to read with

Thy nose like the Tower of Lebanon,
Looking out towards Damascus.

6 Thy head upon thee is like Carmel,
And thy flowing locks like purple—
A king is bound captive in the tresses!

7 How fair—and what a charm hast thou,
Oh love, among delightsome things!

SOLOMON

8 This thy stature is like a palm tree,
And thy breasts like clusters;

9 I think—I will ascend the palm tree,
I will take hold of the boughs thereof.
Oh! may thy breasts be as clusters of the vine,
And the breath of thy nose like apples.

10 And thy palate like the best wine—

SHULAMITE

Flowing for my beloved as his right[1],
Lightly gliding over lips and teeth—

11 I am my beloved's, and to me is his desire.

(d) VII. 12—VIII. 4

SHULAMITE

12 Come, my beloved, let us go forth into the country,
Let us lodge in the villages.

13 Let us get up early to the vineyards,
Let us see whether the vine has budded, the grape-blossom
opened—
Whether the pomegranates are in flower.
There will I give thee my caresses.

---

the Targum בַּת = בֵּית. This word is three times written *defective* on the
Mesha stone, lines 27, 30 *bis* (Driver, *Notes on Sam. lxxxviii.*; *Ges. K.* 7.
2 f.). The words would then mean "the house of many" = "the populous
city of Heshbon."

[1] "מֵישָׁרִים, acc. adv. wie Ps. lviii. 2, lxxv. 3, sicher *mit Recht* nicht *auf-
richtig*. Das Wort bedeutet wie צֶדֶק und מִשְׁפָּט ebensogut ein *Rechthaben*
wie ein *Rechtthun*," Budde on i. 4.

14 The mandrakes diffuse perfume,
   And over our doors are all manner of precious fruits[1],
   New as well as old,
   Which, my beloved, I stored up for thee.
VIII 1 Oh, that thou wert like a brother to me,
   That sucked the breasts of my mother—
   If I found thee outside, I would kiss thee,
   And they would not despise me.
2 I would lead thee, bring thee to my mother's house,
   I would give thee to drink of spiced wine,
   Of the new wine[2] of my pomegranates—.
3 Oh, that his left hand were under my head,
   And that his right hand did embrace me!
4 I adjure you, daughters of Jerusalem,
   Why[3] will ye stir up, and why awaken Love,
   Until it please?

CANTO V. c. VIII. 5—14

(a) VIII. 5—12

THE POET

5 Who is this, coming up from the country,
   Leaning upon her beloved?—

THE BELOVED

Under this apple-tree I waked thee up[4],
There thy mother brought thee forth,
There she brought thee forth that bare thee[4].

---

[1] מְנָדִים here is equivalent to פְּרִי מְנָדִים, iv. 13, 16.

[2] עָסִים. So Is. xlix. 26; Joel i. 5, iv. 18; Amos ix. 13; Vulg. *mustum.* See Del. *Com.*

[3] מָה in this place has been considered to be a negative. *Ges. K.* 137 b, note 1. Graetz. Certainly this particle has almost this sense in Job vi. 11, xvi. 6, xxxi. 1. Still there must be some reason for the substitution of מָה for אִם as in ii. 7, iii. 5, and this passage does not, like those, require so absolute a prohibition.

[4] Reading יְלָדַתֶּךָ, אִמֶּךָ, חִבְּלָתֶךָ, עוֹרַרְתִּיךָ with the Pesh. and nearly all editors.

C. 8

SHULAMITE

6 Set me as a signet-ring upon thy heart,
   As a signet-ring upon thine arm.
   For love is mighty as Death,
   Ardent love as strong as Sheol.
   Its flashes are flashes of fire[1],
   Its fire-flames, fire-flames from Yah[2].
7 Many waters cannot quench love,
   And torrents cannot sweep it away;
   If a man should give
   All the wealth of his house for love,
   Men would surely despise him!—
8 "We have a little sister, and she has no breasts,
   What shall we do for our sister
   In the day when she shall be asked in marriage[3]?
   If she be a wall,
   We will build upon her a silver battlement;
   But if she be a door,
   We will enclose her with a cedar plank."
10 I was a wall,
   And my breasts like towers;
   Then was I in his eyes like one that finds peace.
11 Solomon had a vineyard at Baal Hamon,
   He let out the vineyard unto keepers,
   Every one for the fruit thereof was to bring a thousand
       pieces of silver.
12 My own vineyard is in my power[4];
   The thousand for thee, Solomon,
   And two hundred for the keepers of the fruit.

---

[1] The accents are corrected to רִשְׁפֵּי אֵשׁ. See Wickes, *Heb. Prose Acc.*
p. 138.

[2] Ben Asher read שַׁלְהֶבֶתְיָה (one word), so the Masora. Ben Naphtali,
שַׁלְהֶבֶת יָהּ (two words), Baer, pp. 51, 83. Ginsburg, *Crit. Intr.* p. 386. The
LXX. φλόγες αὐτῆς suggests a plural form. Ewald's fine conjecture

שַׁלְהַבְתֶיהָ שַׁלְהֲבֹת יָהּ

is adopted here.

[3] For this rendering see 1 Sam. xxv. 39; Driver's *Notes on Sam.*, p. 158.
See also Judg. xiv. 7.

[4] For לְפָנָי in this sense see Gen. xxiv. 51, xlvii. 6; 2 Chron. xiv. 6.

(b)   13, 14

THE BELOVED

13 Oh thou that dwellest in the gardens,
The companions are listening for thy voice,
Let me hear it!

SHULAMITE

14 Run away my beloved,
And be like a gazelle or a young hart,
Upon spicy mountains.

EXCURSUS I

ON THE LXX. TEXT OF CANTICLES

The materials available for use in criticising the Heb. text of the Canticles in the light of the Greek versions consist of

1. The four great uncial bibles אABC. The text of B is printed with the variants of the other three in Swete's edition of the LXX.[1]

2. The extant remains of Origen's Hexapla including the Syro-Hexaplar version[2].

3. The readings of other Greek MSS. given by Holmes and Parsons[3].

The Græco-Ven. MS., valuable as it is for renderings, cannot be considered of any value for textual purposes, as it always adheres strictly to the Masoretic text[4] and is therefore no help in the task of getting behind that text, which in the O.T. is the object of all critical enquiry. Nor have we the help of Lucian's Recension, as the groups of MSS. which exhibit that recension[5] do not include the Canticles.

In the use of these materials some process of sifting is required in order to make sure that any reading really represents a divergent form of Hebrew Text read by the Greek translator. In order to do this, it is necessary in the first place to eliminate such variants as have the appearance of originating merely with the translator[6]. For example, δεῦρο in iv. 8 may either be taken as a paraphrastic translation of אִתִּי, or, by changing the vowels, as the imp. fem. of אתה. As it may be taken either way it is not necessarily a various reading.

In another group of readings, where what might seem a various reading in B is not supported by the other three great uncial MSS., it

[1] *The O.T. in Greek according to the LXX.* by H. B. Swete, D.D. Camb. 1891. Vol. II. pp. 506—518. Part of C is missing.

[2] *Origenis Hexaplorum quae supersunt.* F. Field, A.M. Oxf. 1875. Vol. II. 411—424.

[3] In their LXX. Oxf. 1823 etc. Tom. III. ΑΣΜΑ.

[4] "Nunquam consulto, ubi ab Heb. textu discrepat." Græcus-Venetus, ed. O. Gebhardt. Lips. 1875, præf. p. lviii.

[5] Driver, *Notes on Samuel,* p. li. Swete, *Introd. to O.T. in Gr.* p. 83.

[6] Driver, p. xl.

must be carefully considered whether the supposed variant is not a mere error of the somewhat careless scribe of B[1]. Some cases of this kind are

i. 5, δέρρις (א δέρρεις as Exod. xxvi. 7);

i. 13, 14, the omission of the long passage from ἀνὰ μέσον tο ἐμοί (read by אAC), evidently a mere *homoioteleuton*;

ii. 9, ἔστηκεν omitted (= עוֹמֵד read by אAC 23 and a number of other MSS.);

iv. 10, ἀδελφή μου νύμφη ὅτι ἐκαλλιώθησαν μαστοί σου omitted (read by אA (C deest)), another obvious *homoioteleuton*.

viii. 10, ὡς omitted (read by אA).

Such evident errors of transcription do not seem to raise even a presumption that a divergence in the Heb. text lies behind them.

A third class of apparent variations in Cant. arises from a cause which is a familiar source of error in the text of the four Gospels, a natural tendency to assimilate passages containing similar collocations of words still closer to one another[2]. It will be convenient to set out a complete list of passages of this kind, which are in length far the most considerable variants in Cant., and cannot have any claim to represent any divergence of reading in the Heb. text.

i. 3, ὑπὲρ πάντα τὰ [C omits τὰ] ἀρώματα instead of טוֹבִים, inserted from iv. 10;

i. 4, εἰς ὀσμὴν μύρων σου, repeated from v. 3;

ii. 9, ἐπὶ τὰ ὄρη Βαιθήλ, a reminiscence of ii. 17,

ἐπὶ ὄρη κοιλωμάτων

(Heb. בֶּתֶר,

Aq. βαθήρ,

Sym. βαιθήρ,

Theod. θυμιαμάτων,

E΄ διχοτομημάτων,

147, 155, 159, κυκλωμάτων[3]);

---

[1] "A patient and rather dull or mechanical type of transcription, subject now and then to the ordinary lapses which come from flagging watchfulness." Hort, N. T. Introd. § 315 end. Tischendorf is more severe on the accuracy of B, "qui et ipse vitiis scateat" (*N. T. Vat. Proleg.* p. xiii.). Speaking of some errors in the Roman edition he observes, "passim dubitari potest utrum codex an editio laboret vitio...tamen hæc quoque satis cum *universa scripturæ Vaticanæ vitiositate* conveniunt." *Ib.* App. p. xvii.

[2] See Scrivener, *Introd. to Criticism of N.T.* p. 12, 3rd ed. "Some of these variations may possibly have been mere marginal notes in the first instance." *Ib.* So Bickell (*Carm. V. T. metrice* Œniponte 1882, p. 104). "Falsis repetitionibus versiones antiquæ adhuc magis scatent quam Textus Masoreticus."

[3] S[1] has the curious reading μαλα(βά)θρ(ου) which according to Field means "the Betel tree," Field, *Hexap.* ii. 415 n. 47. Budde (*Comm.* p. 13) rather favours this reading on the ground that "Was die Parallelstellen bieten viii. 14, iv. 6 spricht für den Namen eines Wohlgeruchs."

118   EXCURSUS I

ii. 13, περιστερά μου, from next line, v. 14;
iii. 1, ἐκάλεσα αὐτὸν καὶ οὐχ ὑπήκουσέν μου, from v. 6 (AC insert this
again at end of iii. 2);
v. 8, ἐν ταῖς δυνάμεσιν καὶ ἐν ταῖς ἰσχύσεσιν τοῦ ἀγροῦ, from iii. 5;
vi. 5, ὡς σπαρτίον τὸ κόκκινον χείλη σου καὶ ἡ λαλιά σου ὡραία, from iv. 3;
vi. 11, ἐκεῖ δώσω τοὺς μαστούς μου σοί, from vii. 12;
viii. 2, καὶ εἰς ταμεῖον τῆς συλλαβούσης με, from iii. 4;
viii. 4, ἐν ταῖς δυνάμεσιν καὶ ταῖς ἰσχύσεσιν τοῦ ἀγροῦ, from iii. 5.

There will not be much difference of opinion as to the spuriousness
of readings of this kind, the mode in which they originated being so easy
to trace. More difficulty may be felt in regard to the other classes of
variation above enumerated, and especially whether in any particular case
we have before us a differing translation only, or evidence of a divergent
text. The readings now to be enumerated, in the opinion of the present
writer, come under the latter head. It is proposed to subject each one of
them to careful examination and endeavour to solve, so far as may be, the
question, often by no means an easy one, "whether the divergent text is
superior or not to the Masoretic text[1]." These readings in Cant. are
neither very numerous nor very important. They often only extend to one
or two words. There is none of that wide divergence which in the books
of Sam. or Jeremiah makes the Greek text almost resemble a different
recension. And the effect of a critical revision of Cant. upon the Masoretic
text must in any event be very slight, whatever be the decision in individual cases.

The following list does not profess to include every case. Many small
variants such as the insertion or omission of ו or καὶ i. 3, ii. 14, iv. 14, 15,
v. 1, 5, the addition of σὺ ii. 14, the insertion of τί i. 10 and of τὰ iv. 10,
the omission of מָה vii. 2 and of אֵף viii. 10, are not discussed as they do
not really affect the sense.

To proceed to the instances:

i. 2, 4, iv. 10, vii. 13, Heb. דֹּדִים with various suff., Gr. μαστοί.

The Greek evidently represents דַּדִּים, a very slight change, but this
reading is senseless when applied to a *man* as in i. 2, 4. The Hebrew gives
an excellent sense if it be translated "caresses, signs of love" (Gr. Ven.
οἵ σου ἔρωτες), and there seems no need for Geiger's theory[2] that the
word דַּדִּים was changed to דֹּדִים from motives of decency, and that this
locution had caused the canonicity of the book to be doubted! The origin
of the Greek is clear and does not require so elaborate a theory. The
Masoretic text is superior and should stand.

i. 4, Heb. מָשְׁכֵנִי. LXX. εἵλκυσάν σε.
       Aq. εἵλκυσόν με.
       Sym. ἕλκε με.

[1] Driver, *Notes on Samuel*, p. xlviii.
[2] *Urschrift* 397—9.

Theod. as LXX.

E′ εἵλκυσάς με.

The LXX. appear to have read מְשָׁכֵךְ, and (with the exception of the suffix) their reading does not involve any divergent consonantal text, while the disagreement of Aq. and Sym. renders their alteration in the vowels of very little moment. As regards the suffix the ך seems to have been taken up by mistake from the following word, and the other versions have not repeated this error. There is no intrinsic excellence in either variant and the Masoretic text must stand.

i. 5, Heb. יְרוּשָׁלַ͏ִם, B Ἰσραήλ, C and 23 Ἰλημ.

Is the reading of B an original reading or a copyist's error? This question is best decided by a consideration of the structure of the whole poem. The "daughters of Jerusalem" have a definite place and function in the action of the poem and are mentioned in it (if this place be included) seven times (i. 5, ii. 7, iii. 5, 10, v. 8, 16, viii. 4). It is therefore hardly likely that in this one place a different and meaningless designation would be used instead. The Masoretic text is superior in sense and should stand, especially in view of the reading of C.

i. 10.   Heb. בַּתּוֹרִים. LXX. ὡς τρυγόνες (C -ος).

Heb. בַּחֲרוּזִים. LXX. ὡς ὁρμίσκοι.

The Greek translator has read כ for ב in both places, an easy error, and one which spoils the sense of the passage.

i. 11.   Heb. תּוֹרֵי. Gr. Ὁμοιώματα.

This is a curious variant, as the Greek translator has translated the same word τρυγόνες in the verse above. He must have read something different here. What was it? Possibly תֹּאַרֵי. In Judg. viii. 18 ὁμοίωμα is used as the equivalent of תֹּאַר and a graphic confusion of א and ו is not unlikely, or א may have been omitted by later scribes[1]. The only difficulty is that the plural of תֹּאַר is not extant. The Mas. text is obviously right, the Gr. does not give a tolerable sense.

i. 16, Heb. אַף־עַרְשֵׂנוּ רַעֲנָנָה.

LXX. πρὸς κλίνη ἡμῶν σύσκιος (Aq. εὐθαλής).

(C. 70, 106, 147, 149 omit πρός.)

The Greek translator seems to have read אֶל for אַף, again an easy error. There is no reason to alter the Masoretic text.

ii. 4, Heb. הֱבִיאַנִי and דִּגְלוֹ.

LXX. εἰσαγάγετε (-τω 296) and τάξατε.

Aq. ἔταξεν.

Sym. ἐπισωρεύσατε.

These readings do not involve any divergent consonantal text. Presumably the Greek translators read הֲבִיאַנִי and דִּגְלוּ. There is nothing to recommend this variant.

1 Ginsburg, Crit. Introd. p. 137.

ii. 5. Heb. אֲשִׁישׁוֹת. Gr. μύροις.

The key to this variant is probably to be found in 1 Chron. xvi. 3 where ἀμορείτην is used as the equivalent of אֲשִׁישָׁה. This leads to the conclusion that the original Gr. reading was ἀμόραις, in which case there would be no original difference of text.

ii. 10, Heb. קוּמִי לָךְ and וּלְכִי־לָךְ.

LXX. ἀνάστα ἐλθέ and περιστερά μου.

This is a perplexing case. The Hebrew verse is perfectly satisfactory and there is no internal evidence of corruption. The difficulty is to account for the Greek reading. Probably the translator read or pointed לָךְ as לְכִי, and then finding another לכי at the end of the sentence and not requiring another ἐλθέ, which would have been redundant, dropped the two last words. περιστερά μου was probably originally a marginal gloss or reminiscence from the string of words in c. v. 2.

In v. 13 περιστερά μου may have originated in the same way, or may have caught the copyist's eye in the first word of v. 14.

In both cases there is no reason for altering the Masoretic text.

ii. 15, Heb.[1] שׁוּעָלִים שְׁעָלִים.

LXX. ἀλώπεκας (253 bis).

The reading of the LXX. does not represent the universal Greek tradition. "Syro-Hex. in margine notat, Secundum Or. et LXX. et omnes reliquos similiter bis ἀλώπεκας[2]." The Vulg. supports the LXX. while the Pesh. follows the Hebrew. On the whole there is not a sufficient weight of evidence to alter the Masoretic text, which in itself is quite satisfactory.

iii. 11, Heb. בְּנוֹת־צִיּוֹן. Gr. B omits

A θυγατέρες Σιω

after Σολομών א[C, A]　,,　Σιών

C deest.

On this evidence it is clear that the original Greek text did not read these words. Can a reason be suggested for this omission? Probably it arose from the proximity of the words בְּנוֹת יְרוּשָׁלָם and a belief that the two were synonymous. The judgment on this reading will really depend on the interpretation of the passage. It would seem that the "daughters of Jerusalem" (see on i. 5 *sup.*) have a definite place in the machinery of the poem and always mean the same thing, viz. "ladies attached to the Court." The "daughters of Zion" on the other hand seem to mean the women in the streets who are invited to see a procession. If so the words are part of the picture and should not be omitted.

iv. 1, Heb. מֵהַר גִּלְעָד. LXX. ἀπὸ τοῦ Γ.

Sym. ἐξ ὄρους τοῦ Γ'.

[1] The Masoretic text writes the first *plene*, the second *defective*; see Baer, *Quinque volumina*, p. 46.

[2] Field, *Hexap.* ii. 415 n. 36.

This is a notable variant, especially as the Heb. in the parallel place
(vi. 5) reads מִן־הַגִּלְעָד with the Gr.   According to the Onomasticon Galaad
was the name both of a mountain and a district[1], and there is no reason
why the mountain should be referred to rather than the country.   The
Hebrew poet seems to have wished to repeat the hemistich iv. 1 b as closely
as possible in vi. 5 b (including the very rare word גלשו), and it is therefore
hardly likely that he should have introduced a variation in the last words,
and the error might easily arise in transcription; on the whole the Greek
is the reading to be preferred.

iv. 4, Heb. שְׁלְמֵי. LXX. βολίδες.

The Greek translator must have read שְׁלְחֵי, but as the word is an
explanation of אֵלֶף הַפֶּגֶן the Masoretic text is superior and should stand.

iv. 9. Heb. לְבַבְתִּנִי bis. Gr. Ἐκαρδίωσας ἡμᾶς (bis).

Here there is a graphic confusion of ו for י. It is a mere error and
has nothing to recommend it, and the same may be said of iv. 16. μου
י_ read for יְ.

iv. 10, Heb. שְׁמָנַיִךְ. BA ἱματίων.

א μύρων.

The Greek translator appears to have had a text which read שַׂלְמֹתַיִךְ
from v. 11 in error. There is no reason to alter the Masoretic text.

iv. 12, Heb. גַּל. LXX. κῆπος 2°.

The Hebrew text is suspicious. The word גַּל in the singular never
means anything but "a heap of stones[2]" (Gen. xxxi. 46 sqq., Jos. vii. 2,
6, 2 Sam. xviii. 17, Job viii. 17, Is. xxv. 2, all the instances).   In the
plural it often means "the rolling waves of the sea" as "all thy breakers
and thy rollers went over me" (Ps. xlii. 8, Jonah ii. 4).   Such a word, even
if it could mean "wave" in the singular, would be most inappropriate.
Who would call a well in a garden "a locked up wave"? גַּן נָעוּל on the
other hand is most suitable and actually appears in the verse.   The author
of the poem in other places does repeat his expression to gain emphasis
(ii. 15, iv. 1, vii. 1) and may very well have done so here.   This reading
has the support of the Vulg. hortus and of the Pesh. gannᵉtho.   There
is no trace of any Greek variant.   This Greek reading may be confidently
adopted.

iv. 13, Heb. רִמּוֹנִים. LXX. (BאA) omit ῥοῶν, which appears to be

---

[1] Galaad mons...est autem ad tergum Phenices et Arabiæ collibus Libani
copulatus, extenditurque per desertum usque ad eum locum ubi trans Jordanem
habitavit quondam Seon, rex Amorræorum. Lagarde, Onom. 157, 252. Manaim
in tribu Gad separata Levitis in regione Galaaditide. Ib. 170, 275.

[2] Hitzig (Comm. p. 61) adduces the word גֻּלָּה (Josh. xv. 19) which does mean
"spring." But it is enough to say that this is a different word and does not
affect this statement.

supplied by later hands in אA[1]. It is also omitted by 68, 106, 155, 252, 296. "Syr. Hex. in text. παράδεισοι πάντες *ῥοῶν ﹤. Vox ῥοῶν deest in Codd. III. 68. 106 necnon in Latinis Origenis[2]." The quotation in Origen reads "Emissiones tuæ paradisus[3]." This omission is probably deliberate and arises out of difficulties in the exegesis of the passage which are discussed in our note on פַּרְדֵּס[4]. If this be so, there can be no ground to depart from the Masoretic text.

iv. 15. Heb. גַּנִּים. LXX. κηπου B, κηπους אA.

There is little to be said either way as to this variant, as both readings mean much the same thing.

v. 1, Heb. יַעְרִי. LXX. ἄρτον μου.

Sym. δρυμόν.

In view of the reading of Sym. it may perhaps be conjectured that the original LXX. reading was ἀγρόν of which ἄρτον is a corruption. There is no need to disturb the Masoretic text.

v. 2, Heb. דּוֹפֵק. LXX. κρούει ἐπὶ τὴν θύραν, not so (apparently) the Hexaplar writers.

Some help in considering this passage may be gained from Jud. xix. 22, the only other place where the verb דפק is found in the O.T. in this sense. In the latter passage it is followed by עַל־הַדֶּלֶת, LXX. κρούοντες ἐπὶ τὴν θύραν. In view of this it is reasonable to suppose that the words have fallen out of the Hebrew text. They improve the sense and the Greek reading may be adopted.

v. 6, Heb. חָמַק. LXX. omits.

Aq. ἔκλινεν.

Sym. ἀπονεύσας.

On this evidence it seems clear that the word has been omitted from the LXX. by a copyist's error.

v. 11, Heb. כֶּתֶם פָּז.

LXX. χρυσίον, καὶ φὰζ	BA
κεφαζ	א
καιφαζζ	23
καιφαζ	155
Ωφαζ	253
Οφαζ	300

This reading of the LXX. is a compound of καί and a transliteration of פָּז. The variants suggest a reading וּפָז. [Could it be אוּפָז, Jer. x. 9, LXX. Μωφας, or Dan. x. 5, LXX. Ωφαζ? But this word seems itself to be a corruption of Ophir[5], which is too far from the Hebrew text.] The

---

[1] See Swete in loc.

[2] Field II. 418 n. 31.

[3] (Ruff. interp.) Orig. op. ed. De la Rue, III. 65 D.

[4] Exc. III, sub fin.

[5] See Orelli, Com. Jer., ad loc.

two Hebrew words are in apposition[1], and give an excellent sense without
the ‎ו‎. Probably the Greek translator thought the conjunction necessary
and added its equivalent καὶ to improve (to his mind) the sense. The
Masoretic text should stand.

v. 13, Heb. ‎עֲרוּגַת...מֶגְדִּלוֹת‎.

LXX. φιάλαι...φύουσαι.

Aq. and Sym. πρασιαί.

The Greek implies the readings ‎עֲרֻגוֹת‎ (written ‎עֲרֻגוֹת‎ in vi. 2) and
‎מְגַדְּלוֹת‎ (part. Piel as in 2 Kings x. 6). φιάλαι is however difficult to
understand and the original Greek reading was probably πρασιαί as Aq.
and Sym. This gives a much better sense than the Hebrew (which is
indeed very difficult to translate) and is supported by the Vulgate areolœ
consitœ. A plur. noun also agrees better with ‎לְחָיָו‎, and is in fact rendered
necessary by it. The Greek reading may be confidently adopted.

vi. 6, Heb. ‎רְחֵלִים‎. LXX. κεκαρμένων.

This is clearly an assimilation to iv. 2 where the same word is used to
translate ‎קְצוּבוֹת‎. As we have already seen a clear case of assimilation in
vi. 5 from iv. 3, there is no difficulty in pointing to the same phenomenon
here. Ewald[2] thinks that the reading of the Hebrew here is "nur eine
alte Erklärung" of that in iv. 2, and that the LXX. read ‎קְצוּבוֹת‎ in both
places. But the parallel places, iv. 1 f. and vi. 5 f., are not verbally the
same throughout, and the Masoretic text is to be preferred.

vi. 12. There is a very curious variant on this verse, preserved in a
fragment of Origen[3] as follows :

Πατὴρ Νααασὼν ὁ ἄρχων τοῦ λαοῦ μου ᾽Αμιναδὰβ ἔθετό με ἑαυτοῦ εἰς ἅρ-
ματα.

Apparently, whoever was responsible for this reading had no idea what
Aminadib (which he read as one word and as a proper name) meant. He
therefore endeavoured to help out the meaning with a gloss from 1 Chron.
ii. 10 ᾽Αμειναδὰβ ἐγέννησεν τὸν Νααασὼν ἄρχοντα τοῦ οἴκου ᾽Ιούδα, which
perhaps at first was only a marginal note. Such a reading has no critical
value, but is useful as shewing how puzzled the Greek translator was by
this obscure word.

vii. 1, Heb. ‎שׁוּלַמִּית‎, bis.

B   Σουμανεῖτις, so 68.

       Σωμανιτις, 23, 253.

אA   Σουλαμιτις, so 106, 147, 157, 159, 161, 248, 296, 300.

       Σουλαμνιτις, 254.

Syr. Hex. Shilomitho.

---

[1] So Delitzsch, *Com.* Eng. trans. 1891, p. 100.
[2] *Dichter* III. 355 n. 3.
[3] Excerpta Procopiana ex Orig. *opp.* ed. De la Rue, III. 101 B.

Vulg.   Sulamitis.

Sym.   ἡ ἐσκυλευμένη.

Aq. and E′ εἰρηνεύουσα.

It is usual to regard the reading of B as a copyist's error (μαν for ναμ) of that careless scribe.

If this be accepted the key to the variant would seem to be found in the fact that the place Shunem changed its name in later days and became known as Shulem[1], which fact might easily lead to confusion between the two forms. *Riedel*, however, who has given special attention to this variant, thinks that the reading of B indicates a historical interpretation of the poem. He observes[2], "Es wird also die L. A von B, Σουμανεῖτις die ältere und ursprüngliche von G sein. Durch diese Form des Namens soll aber die Braut des Salomo wahrscheinlich mit der Abisag 1 Reg. i. 3 identifiziert werden, denn hier lesen die Handschriften von G durchweg Σουμανεῖτις für Heb. שונמית. Das ist aber eine bestimmte historische Deutung des H. L." But, be this as it may, the evidence against the reading of B is far too strong. How that reading arose is a matter of curious speculation, and perhaps the right explanation may not yet have been found, but it is clear that it cannot displace the Masoretic text.

vii. 1. LXX. inserts ἡ ἐρχομένη for which there is no equivalent in the Hebrew. The latter gives an excellent sense, and it weakens the poem to describe as "coming" one who is already there. Though supported by the Pesh.—*d'nochto*—this variant has no claim to be admitted into the text. The same may be said of LXX. σου at the end of *v.* 7 which simply spoils the sense, and a like case at end of viii. 2.

vii. 10, Heb. דוֹבֵב שִׂפְתֵי יְשֵׁנִים.

LXX. ἱκανούμενος χείλεσίν μου καὶ ὀδοῦσιν.

All the efforts of the commentators to extract a good sense out of the Hebrew reading have proved anything but satisfactory. It is hard to think of any class of persons who would derive less satisfaction from good wine than "sleepers," nor would much be gained by substituting יְשָׁנִים, "old men," an idea quite foreign to the sense of the passage. The Greek gives a much more coherent idea, "Lippen und Zähne bieten dem köstliche Weine kein Hindernis, sie öffnen sich dem süssen Eindringling gern[3]." It is not very easy to see exactly what the Greek translators read. In the first place we may with confidence assume that the true Hebrew reading was ושנים, the very common and easy graphic confusion of י and ו having

---

[1] *Sunem* in tribu Issachar, et usque hodie vicus ostenditur nomine *Sulem*. Lagarde, *Onom.* 183, 284. There is an error in the Greek version Σουβήμ (lege Σουνήμ).

[2] *Die Auslegung des H. L.* Leipzig 1898, p. 106.

[3] Rothstein, *Das Hohe Lied*. Halle 1893, p. 56, n. 2. See Geiger, *Urschrift*, p. 405, who read שְׂפָתַי וִישֵׁנַי, retaining the μου of the LXX.

taken place [1]. We may then provisionally reconstruct the Hebrew thus: שְׂפָתַי וְשָׁנַיִם. This is still not satisfactory, the μου is not wanted in the sentence and rather spoils the sense. The author may have intended a general statement without any personal application. Most likely the original reading of the first word was שְׂפָתַיִם. The Greek reading has the support of both Vulg. and Pesh. and is preferable to the Masoretic text.

viii. 1, Heb. כְּאָח. LXX. omits כ.

No person of taste could accept this variant. The Hebrew is a lovely aspiration, the Greek an absurd and impossible wish.

viii. 2, Heb. תְּלַמְּדֵנִי. LXX. omits (but 23 διδαξῃς με, 147, 157, 159 διδαξεις με).

The word appears to have obelised in the Hexapla, but appears in the Vulgate.

The Hebrew text is most suspicious and the commentators are not agreed as to who is to be the teacher, the *Dōd* or the mother[2]. Here again a marginal gloss is the most likely solution and the word should be omitted from the Masoretic text.

viii. 5, Heb. מִן־הַמִּדְבָּר.

LXX. λελευκανθισμένη, but all Hexaplar versions ἐκ τῆς ἐρήμου.

The only interest of this marvellous variant is to find out how it possibly came about. Delitzsch conjectures[3], "the translator has gathered מִתְחַוֶּרֶת from the illegible consonants of this MS. before him." It is however more probable that he read מִתְבָּרֶרֶת, the Hith. form actually occurs, Dan. xii. 10, and is more like the consonants of the Hebrew text than the word suggested by Delitzsch.

viii. 6[4].

viii. 12, Heb. לָךְ. LXX. omits σοι, 23, 157, 25.

The Hebrew word adds greatly to the force and emphasis of the passage, and should be retained.

This examination (which might be thought by some to be more detailed than is warranted by the results) leads to several conclusions of importance. It is true that the readings adopted from the Greek are few in number, and probably as regards some of these few there will be divergence of opinion as to the propriety of adopting them. It is equally true that if accepted they only affect the Hebrew text to the extent of a word here or a letter there. But the exiguity of these changes may establish a firm conviction that the Masoretic text which lay before the LXX. translators

[1] See list of instances of confusion of yod and waw in Driver, *Notes on Samuel* lxv—lxvii.

[2] See a good note in Oettli, *Comm.* p. 194.

[3] *Comm.* p. 141.

[4] In this passage there are various Heb. readings. It is considered in our note to the translation *supra*.

was (with the exception of assimilative glosses) practically identical with that which we have. Nor is this conclusion at all shaken by what we find in the Hexaplar texts. These it is true avoid the grosser errors of the LXX. (see *e.g.* ii. 7, v. 1, vii. 1, viii. 5), but undoubtedly as a whole they imply the same Hebrew text.

A second conclusion which arises from a study of the Greek variants as a whole is this, that the translators did not very well understand the text they were translating. Such cases as i. 4, ii. 4, vi. 12, viii. 5 might not alone establish this, but to them must be added the gross error twice repeated in the adjuration ii. 7, iii. 5—the mere transliteration of words of which the translator did not know the meaning—θαλπιώθ iv. 4, ἀλὼθ iv. 14, φάζ v. 11, βερατείμ Aq. vii. 6, and most striking of all the translation of geographical proper names. The latter are as follows:

ii. 1, הַשָּׁרוֹן. LXX. τοῦ πεδίου.

iv. 8, מֵרֹאשׁ אֲמָנָה. LXX. ἀπὸ ἀρχῆς πίστεως.

vi. 4, תִּרְצָה. LXX., E′, εὐδοκία, Aq. κατ᾽ εὐδοκίαν, Sym. εὐδοκητή, Theod. and E′ εὐδοκῶ.

vii. 1, שׁוּלַמִּית. Aq. and Sym., see note above.

Ib. הַמַּחֲנָיִם. LXX. παρεμβολῶν.

vii. 5, חֶשְׁבּוֹן. Aq. ἐν ἐπιλογισμῷ[1].

Ib. דַּמָּשֶׂק. Aq. ἀποβλήτων.

viii. 11, בְּעַל הָמוֹן. Aq. ἐν ἔχοντι πλήθη.

Sym. ἐν κατοχῇ ὄχλου.

If the LXX. translators made serious errors in translation, transliterated words they did not understand, and translated proper names like Sharon, Tirzah and Amana, it can only be concluded that they found the text before them either archaic or mystical; and to be either of these it must have been *an old text*. This is not the place to discuss the date of the Song, which has been fully examined in another connection (see section 13 above). But the difficulty which the LXX. and after them the Hexaplar translators found in arriving at its meaning does render impossible any theory which would bring down its date into the Greek age. A work so modern would not have been found so difficult to translate.

It by no means follows because the LXX. affords so little effective help in improving the Masoretic text, that that text is in every respect satisfactory. All that need be said here is that what *we* read, practically the Greek translators read, and if that text is to be improved (if it is in need of improvement) it must be by other methods or by the aid of other materials than are furnished by the Greek versions. (See on this subject Excursus II, *post.*) The fact that the Greek translators found so much

---

[1] This case is more surprising as the place was still in existence in Aquila's day, "*Esebon* civitas Seon...Porro nunc vocatur *Esbus.*" Lagarde, *Onom.* 151, 259.

difficulty in understanding their text may be of service when we come to consider the theory that such text contained Greek loan-words. According to Graetz, Budde and others θαλπιώθ is really a Greek loan-word, τηλῶπις or τηλωπός *a distant prospect*, and the reason the Greek translator did not know its meaning was—because it was a Greek word![1] Most people would think that this was just the reason why one would have expected him to know it. If τηλῶπις had come into the Hebrew language in the Greek age as a Greek loan-word, it was part of the current stock of words, and could hardly have become obsolete when the LXX. version was made. In searching for equivalents, how could he have overlooked a Greek word which so nearly resembled his original and which he must have known? It is not credible. And Aq., Sym. and E′, how could they all have overlooked it? They all translated the word, all differently, and none of the three by τηλῶπις[2]. The variety of their renderings gives a strong impression that they were guessing at the meaning. When this likely word was at their command, how could they fail to find it. Such a state of things is natural enough if the translators had before them an old poem with an archaic Semitic word in it, of which the meaning was lost. It is not what might be expected to occur in translating a new poem written in the Greek age and containing Greek loan-words. The LXX. translator at least, if Cant. were published in the reign of Ptolemy Euergetes (247—221 B.C.), must have been near enough in date to the author to share his circle of ideas as well as his vocabulary. He would have known what תַּלְפִּיּוֹת meant, and if it was really τηλῶπις he must have used that word instead of leaving his original untranslated, especially if that original was barely 100 years old[3].

---

[1] "Zur Zeit dieses Uebersetzers war das Wort nicht mehr bekannt. Warum? Weil es gar nicht hebräisch ist sondern griechisch." Graetz, *Com.* p. 58.

[2] Aq. ἐπάλξεις [so Gr.-Ven.].

Sym. ὕψη.

E′ ἐντολάς.

[3] The LXX. translation seems to have been completed before the prologue of the grandson of Jesus the son of Sirach circa 130 B.C. (Cornill, *Einleit.* 6 ed. p. 320). His words are οὐ γὰρ ἰσοδυναμεῖ αὐτὰ ἐν ἑαυτοῖς Ἑβραιστὶ λεγόμενα καὶ ὅταν μεταχθῇ εἰς ἑτέραν γλῶσσαν· οὐ μόνον δὲ ταῦτα, ἀλλὰ καὶ αὐτὸς ὁ νόμος καὶ αἱ προφητεῖαι καὶ τὰ λοιπὰ τῶν βιβλίων οὐ μικρὰν ἔχει τὴν διαφορὰν ἐν ἑαυτοῖς λεγόμενα. (Swete 2. 644.) "Wenn *talpijoth* ein griechisches Wort gewesen wäre, so würden es die griechischen Uebersetzer wohl erkannt haben." Haupt, *Biblische Liebeslieder*, Anm. 8. 14.

EXCURSUS II

ON CONJECTURAL EMENDATION OF THE
MASORETIC TEXT

It has been shewn in Excursus I that but little improvement of the
Hebrew text of the Song is to be obtained from the Greek Versions. It is
now to be considered whether any help in this direction is to be obtained
by conjectural emendation, and how far it is legitimate. No careful
student of the Masoretic text can consider it uniformly satisfactory. It
is a commonplace of criticism that, while that text was from a certain
period preserved with scrupulous fidelity, there was, prior to that period,
abundant opportunity for corruption, and that corruption has in fact crept
in. Every reader occasionally feels that the passage he is engaged upon
is wrong, and could easily be set right, and, if he gets no help by reference
to the Versions, he is strongly inclined to consider his conjecture as the
original text. Such a process ought however to be most carefully restrained.
The more learned and acute an editor is, the more he is tempted to amend,
and some have allowed themselves such a licence of emendation that they
have made what is almost a new text, and are commenting not on the
Hebrew author but on themselves (see *e.g.* Ps. xvi. in Cheyne's *Psalms*,
2nd ed. I. 50). Such results should suggest the utmost caution in accepting
amendments of the consonantal text on purely subjective grounds. Before
adopting them, every effort should be used to extract a meaning from the
text as it stands. There are, indeed, passages where amendments seem
obvious, and critics almost unanimously admit their necessity. Few
persons would object to such emendations as אַשְׁרֵי for אִמְרוּ Is. iii. 10, or
וְיָבֹם for וְיָבֹא, Is. xli. 25, the latter especially really removes a difficulty
and improves the sense. The prevailing rule, however, should be caution,
as, the bolder is the alteration of text by one critic, the less likely it is
that others, equally learned and acute, will agree with him ; and sound
exegesis will be lost in discussion of texts which, after all, were not written
by the original author, but are, at the best, guesses, more or less brilliant.
Even more to be distrusted are extensive alterations of text which are
made in order to support the editor's views or theories as to history,
geography, ancient religion or the like. Such emendations are often
merely making evidence in support of preconceived theories, and com-
pelling the original author to say what he will not say of himself. It is
safe to affirm that, however attractive such readings may appear for a time,
they will not prove permanent; it is their fate to be dispossessed by
others equally brilliant.

More latitude may perhaps be conceded with regard to alteration of the vowels and accents, which are not part of the original written text. Yet even these are entitled to the greatest respect as representing a very venerable exegetical tradition (see Cheyne, *Psalms*, 2nd ed. I. 10) and as having been preserved by oral repetition only, and yet accurately, for many centuries. While a critic will not hesitate to alter the points in a suitable case, he will not do so unnecessarily or capriciously if he keeps in mind that these points are the best objective evidence he has, or can have, *of what the author meant to write*. In short, "Emendation und Konjektur sind doch immer die *ultima ratio*, die nur denn Platz greift wenn die reiflich erwogene und sorgfältig geprüfte Ueberlieferung den Dienst versagt" (Cornill, *Einleit.* 6th ed. p. 303).

In Canticles many emendations have been suggested which are not unreasonable in themselves, which are supported by the analogy of other passages in O.T. literature, and are not unsuited to the context. But it is conceived that these are not in themselves sufficient reasons for adopting them. Before a conjecture can take the place of the text there ought to be a difficulty which cannot be reasonably solved by exegesis, and there ought to be an evident superiority in the reading proposed. Where there is not a real difficulty, it is submitted that no emendation should be made. It is not enough that the critic should think his reading more striking, more appropriate, or more like some other O.T. passage than the reading in the text, if that reading is not manifestly incorrect. And even then the reading proposed ought to be so suitable, apposite and happy as gradually to win general assent. It ought, in fact, not only to demonstrate the learning and ingenuity of the critic; it should also carry the conviction that it successfully *restores what the author wrote*. Tried by this standard not many emendations (unsupported by any version), in proportion to the number suggested, will be finally and generally adopted, and pure conjecture will be reduced to very narrow limits.

And this general view of the matter will be confirmed when it is considered that a system of interpretation based on extensive emendation has always in fact proved to have less chance of general adoption than any other; such a system is far too subjective and individual to win general assent. Graetz's Commentary (*Schir-ha-Schirim*, 1871) is a monument of learning and industry, its author is of the highest authority, and yet (as far as we know) no other editor has endorsed his theory. Why? Surely because (as will be shown later) he altered the text to make his theory possible. It should be the task of any editor who would wish that his work should convince others, to endeavour to explain the text *as it stands*, with the help of the Versions (especially the Greek Versions), but with the most sparing and careful use of conjectural emendation.

It is interesting to consider the difference in this respect between the older Commentators on the Canticles and those of more recent date. The early editors, *e.g.* Ewald, Hitzig and Delitzsch, applied themselves to the explanation of the text and found little need for emendation. Ewald, indeed, went so far as to say that the poem had been preserved in a relatively extremely pure diction, and that this had been an agreeable surprise to him ("so wurde man eher manche verderbte oder doch weniger ursprüngliche Lesart erwarten, und sieht sich desto angenehmer getäuscht," *Dichter*, II. 355, 2nd Aufl.).

Naturally, taking this view, his proposals for emendation are very few. Similarly Delitzsch, discussing and rejecting a slight emendation on ii. 17, states his rule "We hold by what is written" (*Comm. E. T.* 1891, p. 56). These editors obtained their interpretations from the traditional text, and, whatever may be thought of their results, they were at least arrived at without the extensive alterations and dislocations which lie at the basis of some more modern systems of exegesis. The same may be said of such expositors as Ginsburg, Renan, Robertson Smith, Rothstein, Oettli, Bruston, Kingsbury, the class whom Budde so scornfully styles *Dramatiker*; they did not find it requisite, in order to explain the text, to practically rewrite it.

Later writers have not however used the same restraint or have taken a different view of the functions of an editor. Some of the emendations proposed seem to arise from mere caprice. A few examples of these may be given.

The text of i. 5 is a pretty and poetical antithesis :

> I am black, as tents of Kedar, but
> Comely, as pavilions of Solomon.

Cheyne (*Enc. Bib.*, art. *Salmah*), also Bickell and Winckler, point this last word as שַׁלְמָה, Salmah, the name of an Arabian tribe who lived near Kedar, and who are certainly not wanted here. The change takes all the point out of the passage.

In iv. 6 the text reads

> I will get me to the mount of *myrrh*,
> And to the hill of *frankincense*.

Cheyne (*Enc. Bib.*, art. *Song of Sol.*) proposes to read

חֶרְמוֹן for הַמֹּר, and הַלְּבָנוֹן for הַלְּבוֹנָה.

Why, we cannot conjecture.

In iv. 8 Cheyne (*ubi sup.*) would read for אֲרָיוֹת—אֲרָזִים, and for נְמֵרִים—בְּרֹשִׁים, which is curious, as our author writes this word בְּרוֹתִים (see i. 17). This alteration very much lessens the force of this fine passage and is entirely unnecessary.

It is not likely that emendations of this kind will obtain general assent.

Graetz goes much further and declares plainly that he alters the text in order to make it possible to explain it according to his theory as to its interpretation. He remarks, "Die ganze Fabel vom Raube der Sulamit für den Salamonischen Harem beruht *einzig und allein auf Text-Ver-derbniss,*" which is only another way of saying that it is found in the text, but he will remove it; and again, "In der That zeigt sich in demselben eine ganze Reihe von Text-Verderbnissen und auch bei wesentlichen Punkten, von denen das Verständniss des ganzen abhängt" (*Schir-ha-Schirim*, pp. 100, 101). It will be interesting to see how he deals with those passages which chiefly embarrass him.

i. 4. The importance of this passage in any view of the interpretation of the poem is obvious. Graetz alters the singular suffixes to the plural, reading מָשְׁכֵנוּ and הֱבִיאָנוּ, and by translating *Draw us...if the king would bring us,* obtains the change of meaning he wants.

vi. 12. This is the passage referred to above, and one to which Graetz devotes his whole strength. In his edition the poem is entirely dislocated, the lines are lifted about to all sorts of places, then the words

$$\text{לֹא יָדַעְתִּי נַפְשִׁי}$$

are read together (against the accents) and the remaining words read thus שָׂמַתְּנִי מֶרַד בַּת־עַמִּינָדִיב in the sense

> I do not know myself,
> Thou hast made me soft,
> Daughter of Amminadib!

What a poor insipid result, and yet how cleverly arrived at! But surely no one would think this emendation any improvement on the original text, and probably neither Graetz nor anyone else in the world ever thought that the original poet really wrote the poem in the form to which he has reduced it. It is a very ingenious piece of work by a very acute editor, and it is the sort of thing which is sure to happen when editors begin to rewrite texts to fit them to theories of interpretation. Some illustrations of the same process may be given from K. Budde (*Die Fünf Megilloth*, Tüb. 1898), who is equally ready to alter passages where they are in his way.

Thus, on i. 16 he observes that "Lagern im grüuen Grase...passt freilich besser zu dem Gedenken an den fernen ländlichen Geliebten in Gegensatz zu König Salomo, als der Hochzeit," which is quite true. So, without any grounds, he proceeds to alter רַעֲנָנָה to תַּעֲנֻגָּה, and the hindrance is got rid of.

Then again in vi. 4, where, as is well known, much weight has been laid on the conjunction of *Tirzah* and Jerusalem, Budde thinks the easiest way out is to delete the words כְּתִרְצָה נָאוָה כִּירוּשָׁלָ͏ִם, although he is quite unable to explain how they came to be there, if they were not originally written by the author.

These instances are enough to show how unsound a method of interpretation must be which alters a text with the avowed object of removing objections to a theory of interpretation. It is not to be expected that subsequent editors will take over these alterations: they will rather devise fresh ones of their own in support of rival theories.

An extensive system of rewriting the text may be found in G. Bickell, *Carmina Vet. Test. metrice* (Oeniponte 1882). This author with great learning and ingenuity evolved a metrical system, and in applying it to Canticles he has been obliged in nearly every verse throughout the poem to leave out or to insert one, two, or three words, so as to get the number of feet required by his scheme.

For examples of additions:

i. 7. He reads תַּרְבִּיץ אֲמָצְאַךְ.

ii. 8.   ,,   קוֹל דּוֹדִי שָׁמַעְתִּי, and worse still הִנֵּה זֶה בָּא יָבֹא.

Of omissions

ii. 12. He omits בְּאַרְצֵנוּ at the end.

v. 11.   ,,   רֹאשׁוֹ כֶּתֶם פָּז.

These are specimens of the treatment of the poem throughout in the interests of this metrical theory. But this editor also alters very largely to suit his general views of interpretation. He leaves out altogether nine and a half verses (i. 15, ii. 17, iii. 5, iv. 5, vi. 5 *b* to 8, viii. 3, 4) and a very large number of halves or portions of verses on a general theory, "Generatim omnia in Cant. verbotenus repetita...serius inserta sunt." Further in c. iii. he gives the following remarkable collocation of verses: iii. 6, vi. 10, 11, 12, vii. 1, viii. 5, iii. 7 sq. By this method anything can be made into anything.

Many of Bickell's alterations seem to be the result of mere fancy and caprice. He is troubled by readings which have troubled no one else, and his reasons are extraordinary.

Thus in i. 2—4 among other amendments he omits מִיַּיִן twice,

"Nam uxores Sal. hic inter poculorum commercia more studiosorum Germanicorum carmen conviviale concinnere, prorsus incredibile videtur!"

On i. 11 he alters נַעֲשֶׂה to אֶעֱשֶׂה,

"Non apparet cur amans tanquam e persona plurium de se loquatur."

As if a king would make a necklace with his own hands! It is a plural of regality.

In iv. 4 he alters עָלָיו to בּוֹ,

"Quis suspendet arma in muris exterioribus armamentarii?"

Budde has disposed of this by a simple reference to Ezek. xxvii. 11, 1 Macc. iv. 57.

In v. 7 he omits מְצָאֻנִי הַשֹּׁמְרִים הַסֹּבְבִים בָּעִיר and שֹׁמְרֵי הַחֹמוֹת.

"Num forte barbari aut latrones erant illi custodes Hierosolymorum?"

He actually alters the text because he does not like a detail in a poetic description of the dream of a girl in distress!

In vii. 4 he omits שְׁנֵי.

"Numerus hæc omnino superfluit."

That is a question of taste, and we prefer that of the poet.

And finally he is so good as to supply lines omitted by the author, as

v. 5 e. Supple stichum "Quam stillaverunt manus dilecti mei."

vi. 8 d. Supple stichum "Sunt in gynæceo regis."

These few specimens are enough to show how an editor of this kind practically rewrites the poem. Such a performance produces a double effect on the reader. He cannot help admiring Bickell's learning and ingenuity, and at the same time has no confidence at all in the text he offers. After reading with much interest his emendations one asks, "Am I really convinced that this is what the author wrote?" The answer must be in the negative : "These are merely the clever exercises of the Innsbruck Professor." Neither Graetz nor Bickell has, in regard to text, convinced later editors.

This will be apparent if we return to Budde's *Commentary (sup. cit.)*, of which a not inconsiderable proportion is devoted to refuting the textual suggestions of Graetz and Bickell. And it is not unworthy of remark that for this work Bickell communicated to the editor an *entirely fresh set of readings* from his then unpublished work "Kritische Bearbeitung d. H. L." (Budde, p. xxiv). Some of Budde's remarks are worth quoting.

It has been already pointed out that many of Bickell's emendations are based on the view that every repetition in the poem is an interpolation. Budde (on i. 15) takes a very different view, "Uebrigens kann die Wiederholung gewisser Zeilen und selbst Verse in diesen Liedern an sich nicht auffallen, und braucht keinesweg *überall* auf Eintragung zu beruhen, so sorgsam diese Möglichkeit auch stets in Betracht zu ziehen ist."

Then on v. 7, where Bickell cuts so deep, he remarks, "Bis בָּעִיר gleich iii. 3 a. Dort werden die Wächter nur vergeblich um Auskunft gefragt : hier behandeln sie das Mädchen das sich bei Nacht draussen herumtriebt als eine Verworfene. Das ist ein ganz passender Abschluss, des Traums durchaus würdig, so das dem Inhalt nach *kein Anlass ist den Vers mit Bickell* als späteren Anhang mit übertreibender Benutzung von iii. 3 *zu streichen.*" This extract is typical of a very large number of places where Budde discusses and usually rejects the emendations of Graetz, Bickell, Martineau and others, and the really valuable matter he supplies is obscured by this cloud of textual controversy. In such discussions every one differs from every one else—no one is convinced—Bickell[1] differs from Bickell[2], and there is no hope that unanimity or finality will ever be secured. Thus in vi. 4 b, a passage which presents no difficulty at all to the ordinary reader, Bickell[1] reads only the words כְּתָר תִּרְצָה נָאוָה, striking out the rest of the verse.

Bickell[2] strikes out כְּתִרְצָה נָאוָה כִּירוּשָׁלַם and keeps the rest of the verse. There is not in either reading that evident superiority to the text which convinces subsequent critics, and results in abiding additions to knowledge. Such conjectures only lead to more discussion, more disagreement, and further attempts to amend.

Take again the opening words of viii. 11. There is no reason whatever to suspect the reading *Baal-Hamon* whether it be (as usually) identified with Βαλαμών (Judith viii. 3) near Dothain and Shulem or (Budde) with Jibleam (2 Kings ix. 27). Graetz however proposes בַּעַל חֶרְמוֹן (Josh. xi. 17, xii. 7, Judg. iii. 3, 1 Chron. v. 33), while Bickell[1 and 2] omits בְּבַעַל הָמוֹן altogether. Budde observes that Graetz' reading "gehört gar nicht hieher," and that Bickell's omission is "ohne Grundangabe damals wie jetzt, also nur des Metrums wegen. Damit nimmt er dem Verse Licht und Farbe." Here are three very learned editors with three divergent opinions. How is it possible to do anything but maintain the Masoretic text?

There is no need to multiply further examples of discrepant emendations. The hopeless want of agreement about them confirms the view, which is, *a priori*, a sound one, that no emendation should be accepted which is introduced to support a theory, whether expository or metrical. As regards emendations where there is an acknowledged difficulty in the text and a reasonable degree of assent on the part of expositors, such should be carefully weighed and, if found convincing, accepted. But there are very few such places in Canticles, perhaps the most certain is Ewald's conjecture on viii. 6 (see note in our translation). Many cases of difficulty however on careful consideration will be found to yield an equally good meaning, or to be capable of explanation, without altering the text.

For instance, in i. 3 שֶׁמֶן תּוּרַק שְׁמֶךָ, apart from other difficulties, both of the possible subjects are *masc.* and the verb is *fem.* Many changes have been tried, מוּרָק, יוּרַק, תַּמְרוּק (Graetz from Est. ii. 3—12, a particularly unpleasant suggestion), *Trachonitic*, *Turkish* or *Thracian*! oil (Bickell, תרקי in some such sense) and so on. Is it not however simpler to treat this violation of concord as a provincial irregularity? just as שֶׁמֶשׁ in Jud. xix. 14 is exceptionally feminine, probably from a similar cause. Enallage of genders is a striking feature of the language of Canticles (see Exc. III).

Or take the difficult passage iii. 10,

תּוֹכוֹ רָצוּף אַהֲבָה מִבְּנוֹת יְרוּשָׁלָם.

רצף denotes tesselation, inlaying, mosaic work. What then can be the meaning of "inlaid with love"? אַהֲבָה *dilectam* (Hos. iii. 1) is out of the question, "we cannot speak of being inlaid or tesselated with persons" (Del.). Graetz and Bickell[2] remove בְּנוֹת יְרוּשָׁלָם to the next sentence and substitute, for אהבה, אהבים (a word which does not exist) or הָבְנִים, ebony (Ezek. xxvii. 15 K'ri). Budde after a careful discussion thinks "Eine sichere Entscheidung ist nicht zu geben." Why not then adopt the very reasonable suggestion of Ginsburg that the noun אַהֲבָה may be used adverbially as "lovely, charmingly" (comp. אֹהֲבֵם נְדָבָה, I will love them freely, Hos. xiv. 4)? and translate

Its interior inlaid in lovely fashion
By the daughters of Jerusalem.

In the above two instances the text carefully scanned has yielded as good a sense as any suggested variant.

D. C. Siegfried (*Handkommentar*, Götting. 1898) avoids this constant and irritating alteration of single words, but the changes proposed by him are far from trifling, and generally speaking, so far as they are *omissions*, are in the interest of his interpretation of the text, which is largely the same as Budde's (see sect. 9 *sup.*).

Thus he would omit i. 7, 8 as "ein Stück eines anderen Liebesliedes," which really is a very inadequate reason, as according to him the whole poem is a mosaic of such fragments. His true reason is of course that on his theory of the poem it is impossible to make sense of these verses. It should be observed that *v.* 8 contains a strong proof that it is an integral part of the poem by its use of the phrase הַיָפָה בַּנָּשִׁים, which also occurs in v. 9, vi. 1.

Similarly and for the same purpose he omits the very striking verse, ii. 15, as a gloss "an סְמָדַר in *v.* 13 angeknüpft." As if the poet could not mention the vine-bloom more than once!

Then he omits iii. 4 *c*, *d* as borrowed from viii. 2, and viii. 3, 4 as borrowed from ii. 6, 7 or iii. 5. This horror of repetitions or recurrent phrases is an echo of the absurd principle laid down by Bickell, but it has its use in destroying the structure of the poem, which is one of the most striking proofs of its unity.

The verse iv. 8, again, does not fit into Siegfried's mode of interpretation, so it is pronounced to be "eine auf einem groben Missverstandniss eines spätern Lesers beruhende Glosse." It is somewhat strange that a marginal gloss should produce so striking and original a verse, and one eminently worthy to be compared with anything written by the real author. On the other hand we are grateful to Siegfried that he will have nothing to do with emendation *metri causa*. It is most refreshing to read in his preface, "Zur Heeresfolge in Betreff seines (Bickell's) metrischen Systems habe ich mich nicht entschliessen können. Die Sclaverei in welche bei Bickell der Textkritiker dem Metriker gegenüber gerät, wirkte allzu abschreckend." We hope to give further justification of these wise words as we proceed.

It may be observed that Cornill (*Einleit.* 6th ed.) also proposes to strike out among other passages iv. 8, viii. 3, 4. As his view of the interpretation of the poem agrees with that of Budde and Siegfried, it would seem that it is not possible to maintain that view unless those verses (at least) are removed from the text.

Is the poem then entirely free from glosses? is there no passage which looks like a later addition? In the writer's opinion the verses iii. 9, 10 are somewhat suspicious (see Cheyne, *Enc. Bib.*, art. *Litter*; Rothstein, *Das H. L.* 1893, p. 46). They are extremely prosaic, they break the flow of an animated poetic scene, and *v.* 11 follows naturally on *v.* 8. As however these verses are found in all the versions, it is perhaps safer not to pronounce them definitely spurious but doubtful. We have therefore retained them in the translation, but enclosed in brackets. With this exception we are unable to see that any other verse in the poem is out of place or unworthy to be considered the work of the original poet.

There is another way of considering the value of critical emendation which has hardly received the amount of attention it deserves. Much has been said by emendators as to the interpretation of the poem, as to suggested repetitions, as to metre, but these are by no means all the questions involved. It ought also to be considered how this critical handling affects the *literary value* of the poem: questions of taste and fitness are involved. If "slashing Bentley with his desperate hook" is to be let loose on a literary masterpiece, the results can hardly be justified unless the beauty of the work is enhanced by the process. If the emendator with happy skill removes obscurities, brings out the beauty of the poem, adds to its charms, increases its claims to admiration, and, above all, is careful not to remove or impair its most characteristic excellences, he does a service to literature and his work is likely to prove of permanent value. But how few emendations come up to this standard; how many will fail of obtaining the universal approval of people with a trained literary sense. Let us consider the latest serious attempt to produce a revised standard text of the Canticles, that of G. Dalman (in *Biblia Hebraica*, ed. R. Kittel, Lips. 1905). In this edition besides emendations based on the versions or on other grounds, about sixty passages or words are proposed to be omitted *metri causa*. Few readers will peruse these omissions without a feeling of astonishment that the editor has had no difficulty in parting with some of the most charming and characteristic touches in the poem, simply because they would not fit into his metrical structure. It is hard to think that any reader who has been accustomed to taste the beauties of this lovely poem will consent to part with these passages.

For example, in i. 4 we are to omit the words מֵישָׁרִים אֲהֵבוּךָ, the culmination of the praises of the Chorus, "*they are in the right who love thee,*" a fine poetic phrase suitable to the occasion and causing no difficulty in interpretation. Who would part with these words in the interests of a metrical theory?

Worse still in i. 6 the touching and beautiful phrase—כַּרְמִי שֶׁלִּי לֹא נָטָרְתִּי is to go. There is perhaps no passage in the poem more attractive than this; if it does not fit the metre it fits the sense. "They appointed me to guard the vineyards, *but I did not guard the vineyard which was my own.*" How could any critic doubt that this passage is original and genuine? These very words, so appropriate to the sombre beginning of the poem, recur in its triumphant close (viii. 12), כַּרְמִי שֶׁלִּי לְפָנָי, "My vineyard, still my own, is in my power," and thus the poem is in harmony with itself.

And in i. 8 why are we to lose the words, עַל מִשְׁכְּנוֹת הָרֹעִים? Surely they are appropriate to the sense. "If thou dost not know (where thy lover is shepherding his flocks) go out on the heels of the sheep and feed thy kids"—Where? *By the shepherds' dwellings.* It is part of the sarcasm that she who dreads to wander among the shepherds, must do so to find her lover, if she is so foolish as to love a shepherd. These words are required by the sense.

And why are we to lose the pretty repetition in i. 15 and iv. 1, הִנָּךְ יָפָה? It is a characteristic beauty of the poem. Even worse is the omission of the first לְבַבְתִּנִי in iv. 9. Must all emphasis be taken away *metri causa*? What is more natural than this? *Thou hast made me bold, my sister betrothed, thou hast made me bold.* It would be a poor frigid rule of criticism which would allow a poet no repetitions, and such a rule would destroy most of the masterpieces of English lyric poetry.

We now turn to three passages where the critic adopts a somewhat novel method of settling a text: he offers alternatives of deletion.

In ii. 10, עָנָה דוֹדִי וְאָמַר לִי, he observes *extra met. (vel del.?)*. But these words are indispensable, and the critic evidently feels this. *My beloved has begun to speak to me,* and then the poet goes on to quote what he says. Metre or no metre, the words cannot be deleted.

In iii. 9 the choice is offered to omit either שְׁלֹמֹה or הַמֶּלֶךְ. Until it is settled by some substantial argument *which* ought to go, there is nothing for it but to retain both.

In iii. 11 a similar alternative is offered, either to omit בְּיוֹם חֲתֻנָּתוֹ or if preferred וּבְיוֹם שִׂמְחַת לִבּוֹ.

This is really too much. There is not in the whole poem a stronger or more original passage than this. The crown on the head of King Solomon has a special significance. It commemorates not only his marriage (which was hardly an unique event in his life) but also a marriage with some joyful association attached to it. It recalls "*the day of his marriage, and the day of his heart's delight.*" This fine ringing phrase is both beautiful in itself and of value in interpretation. Neither half of it can be spared.

How any person of taste could wish to leave out the whole verse, v. 7, we are at a loss to understand. The opinion of Budde on this passage has already been quoted, and it is only needful here to point out how suitable the words are to the dream of a girl in distress. "*The watchmen going round in the city found me, they beat me, they wounded me; they took my veil off me, did the watchmen of the walls.*" Does anyone really think that these words were not written by the original author?

Again it is an extraordinary want of taste which would leave out in vi. 8 the concluding words וַעֲלָמוֹת אֵין מִסְפָּר. As Graetz pointed out, the poet is drawing out an effective comparison between the harem of Solomon and one country girl. *They are 60 queens and 80 concubines, and girls— not to be counted. She is ONE.* It is not a numerical comparison between 140 and 1: that would be very poor in poetry. It is a contrast between an innumerable host and one. Consider too that these, עֲלָמוֹת, have already been referred to in i. 3 as the sort of persons who love Solomon. The omission of these words would spoil the passage.

Another very strange omission is to be found in ii. 5, amounting to real mutilation, כִּי חוֹלַת אַהֲבָה אָנִי. She asks to be sustained with grape cakes and revived with apples, a meaningless statement unless the reason followed. *Because I am sick with love.* How can these words be omitted? They are absolutely necessary.

An almost test place may be found in the proposal to omit, in vii. 13, שָׁם אֶתֵּן אֶת־דֹּדַי לָךְ, a delicate and beautiful touch. Let us for a moment try to realise the situation. The girl will soon be free, the divided lovers will soon meet and start on the journey home. She pictures the open country, the lodging in villages, the vineyards, the scene of their early happiness (ii. 4). *There*, not in the streets of the hateful city, not in the strange villages, or the unfamiliar plain, but in the places where we have been happy before and hope to be happy again, *there I will bestow my caresses upon thee.* These words are no interpolation, they justify themselves to the taste and the feelings. If anyone wishes to see what these words look like when they *are* interpolated let him glance at the LXX. of vi. 11.

Once more, in viii. 13 it is proposed to omit the words חֲבֵרִים מַקְשִׁיבִים, a fine and delicate touch. *The companions are listening for* thy voice. Let *me* hear (it). If you will not sing for my friends, oh! sing for me as you did under very different circumstances (ii. 14). Why should we lose the phrase which so suitably introduces this thought.

These alterations are only specimens of many others; hardly one of the 60 proposed omissions really commends itself as an improvement, and nearly every one of them is a distinct loss, removing from the poem either some touch of beauty or some delicate aid to interpretation.

Now if these 60 phrases are interpolations they must have been deliberately added by some person, for some purpose. By what sort of person and for what purpose? Who is this unknown redactor or glossator, who goes through a poem, adding delicate and graceful touches, just where they will add to the beauty of the whole, utterly disregarding the metre as he improves the poetical expression? Did such an one not know that the poem was written on a strict metrical system, or, knowing it, had he no scruples about spoiling it? Such questions of course cannot be answered, and yet some intelligible theory ought to be brought forward to account for the existence of these passages in the poem, before they are rejected merely because they cannot be chopped into lengths, and measured with a foot-rule. As a whole they must be approved on grounds of taste and poetic fitness; are they to be rejected merely on the ground of metric theory? Do we, in fact, really come to the conclusion that they were no part of the original poem; or does the critic only mean (as he expressly says of the words in ii. 10) that they are *extra metrum*, and that *if* his metrical theory is correct, they cannot be made to fit in with it?

But no proposition as to Hebrew metre can be considered sufficiently settled to justify editors in moulding a text to any metrical system. (See König, *Stilistik, Rhetorik u. Poetik*, Lips. 1900, pp. 309—46.) If anything could be considered certain on this uncertain subject it would seem to be that *metre* as known in European poetry is not to be found in Hebrew, that the number of syllables in a *stichos* or verse is immaterial, and that the essential element in Hebrew poetry is found in the accents or *ictûs*, of which there may be varying numbers in different verses. The lines in a verse may be longer or shorter as the poet may desire, nor is there any necessity that the lines composing a verse should all be of the same length. (See Cornill, *Einleit.* 6th ed., 10—17; Driver, *Introd.* 8th ed., 361 fol.) If this be the case, if the *foot* as such is not the element to be sought but the *rhythmic beat*, it is hard to feel any confidence in any system of emendation which removes considerable portions of the text to obtain an equal number of feet in every line.

We have now reviewed, with very little satisfaction, several systems of conjectural emendation, and have found that whether they arise from mere ingenuity, or from a desire to support an exegetical theory, or from attempts to work out a metrical system, they all in common present these features :

(*a*) They do not improve but injure the poem from a literary point of view.

(*b*) They are mutually self-destructive in their divergence from each other, and absence of even approximate agreement.

(*c*) They fail to produce in the mind a feeling of obviousness and certainty—"this is undoubtedly what the author wrote."

In fact, as these extensive schemes are scanned, as each passage of the traditional text is compared with these various and conflicting substitutes, it emerges superior to any of their divergent proposals in nearly every case.

The writer, after carefully examining such schemes of emendation, has arrived at the conclusion that as yet no better way of dealing with this difficult text has been found, than a serious effort to extract if possible a reasonable sense out of the traditional text, judiciously corrected with the aid of the Versions. It is his belief, that if this method be pursued, the number of purely conjectural emendations ultimately adopted will not be many, and that a careful consideration in each case, with a view of deciding whether the proposed reading is *manifestly superior* to the text, will lead to a large agreement with Ewald's view that that text is on the whole pure and well preserved. This is not questioning the fact that the interpretation of this poem is a task of extraordinary difficulty. Least of all will anyone who has essayed the task of interpretation minimise the difficulty. But the writer feels strongly that those interpretations which rest on extensive alterations of text are desperate expedients. The editors who adopt such a system have renounced the explanation of the poem, and are explaining something else. It is not to be thought that such a system can ultimately give satisfaction or lead to finality, or that an enduring exegesis can be built up on the shifting and insecure basis of subjective criticism.

Since these pages were written the writer has seen the work *Biblische Liebeslieder*, von Paul Haupt (Leipzig and Baltimore, 1907), which affords some striking illustrations of the views expressed above. This author has gone far away from Budde or Siegfried. He cannot find the *threshing wain*, which is the pivot of their theory, in the poem at all; nor does he think the poem is the text-book of a Judean wedding, or anything but a mass of mutilated fragments. It is "eine nach Beginn des Seleuciden Ära (312 v. Chr.) in Damaskus (!) zusammengestellte Sammlung volkstümlicher hebräischer Hochzeits- und Liebeslieder, die alle bei Hochzeiten gesungen worden sein können, *wenn sie auch zunächst nicht für diesen Zweck verfasst waren*," p. xiii. Haupt has set himself to restore these original poems, and, by striking out a large portion of the existing text and dislocating what is left, he has produced twelve songs or broken fragments of songs; occasionally filling up a lacuna with a line of his own.

Song I. is composed of iii. 6—11.

„ II. of vi. 9—vii. 9.

„ III. of vi. 2, vii. 10, ii. 1, i. 5, 6, viii. 8, 9, 10, 1, 2.

„ IV. of viii. 11, 12, vi. 7, 8.

„ V. of iv. 8.

„ VI. of v. 2—16.

„ VII. of i. 16, 17, ii. 3—6, i. 12—14, 2, 3, 4, 16, 17, 7.

„ VIII. of iv. 1—4, i. 9, 10, iv. 5, 7, vi. 3, 4, iv. 9—15, 13, 14, 16.

„ IX. of iv. 17, vii. 11, 12, 13, vi. 10, v. 1, vi. 1.

„ X. of ii. 8—14, 2.

„ XI. of i. 7, 8.

„ XII. of iii. 1—4, viii. 6, 7.

The mythical Damascene editor must indeed have been a person of surpassing genius, if he was able (in a language not his own) to produce, out of this disconnected mass of fragments, the lovely poem as it now exists.

Let us see how Song II. is made up:

vi. 9 with the order of lines inverted thus *a, d, b, c.*

(vi. 10 moved to Song IX.)

(vi. 11 struck out as a gloss.)

vi. 12.

vii. 1.

vii. 7 (striking out "A King is bound captive in thy tresses ").

vii. 5.

(vii. 3 struck out as a gloss.)

(vii. 8 struck out as a gloss.)

vii. 4 (striking out "at the gate of Bath-rabbim").

vii. 9 (striking out "flowing for my beloved smoothly").

vii. 2 inverted thus *b, a.*

Out of 12 verses an amount which is at least equal to 4 is struck out, one is moved to another place, and the rest are arranged capriciously.

Or take Song XII. made up thus:

iii. 1 striking out *c,* 4 words.

  „ 2 „   „   *b,* 9 „

  „ 3 „   „   2 „

  „ 4 „   „   9 „

(„ 5 struck out altogether.)

A line by the editor is inserted as follows : " Ich sagte zu meinem Herzliebsten," to join up viii. 6, 7.

This is much the same method as that of Graetz, but carried much further. When Graetz had finished his emendations, there was left a connected poem and something of a story. But this writer has taken all meaning out of the poem, and all his cutting seems merely designed to get a certain number of lines to sort into unconnected *Volkslieder.*

Emendation of this sort has no critical value and no scientific foundation : it will convince no one except its author. Who can believe in these imaginary compilers, who are so readily invented, or in the theories which make it necessary to invent them ? We shall be very much surprised if any future editor adopts Haupt's twelve *Lieder* and their Damascene compiler as an adequate explanation of the phenomena of the Song. Other editors will doubtless arise, equally bold and ingenious, but they will not, we may be certain, adopt either this system or those of Graetz or Bickell. They will prefer their own emendated or rewritten texts, for there is neither progress nor finality in capricious emendation or in theories which are only rendered possible by the free use of it.

Note. The use of *Pas'ek* in Canticles in no way supports the view (*Ges.-K.* 15 f. n.[2], Cheyne, *Psalms,* ed. 2, I. p. lxviii; see Steuernagel, *Einleit.* p. 34) that this sign is any indication of corruption in the text. The eight *Pas'eks* in this book are all easy to account for by the ordinary rules, the one in iv. 12 is obviously *euphonic* (Wickes, *Accents,* p. 124), those in i. 13, i. 14, ii. 7, iii. 5 and viii. 4 are *dichotomic,* and those in ii. 13, iii. 11 *emphatic.*

EXCURSUS III

ON THE LANGUAGE OF CANTICLES

The linguistic peculiarities of this book are numerous and striking. They may be arranged under the following heads.

A. Enallage of genders.

B. Words or forms (including Aramaisms) not found in any other parts of the O.T.

C. Provincialisms.

D. Other Aramaic forms and expressions.

(A) Enallage of genders.

One of the most curious features of the language of Canticles is the frequent substitution of *masc.* for *fem.* forms both in verbs and pronouns. This phenomenon is occasionally found in various parts of Hebrew literature, but is peculiarly marked in our book. Examples are:

   (*a*) *Verbs* i. 6. אַל־תִּרְאֻנִי for אַל־תִּרְאֶינָה אֹתִי.

Similarly ii. 5. רַפְּדוּנִי and סַמְּכוּנִי.

    ,,   ii. 7. תָּעִירוּ and תְּעוֹרְרוּ.

    ,,   v. 8. תִּמְצְאוּ and תַּגִּידוּ.

         v. 9. הִשְׁבַּעְתָּנוּ for יֵנוּ, as iv. 9.

         vii. 1. תֶּחֱזוּ.

   (*b*) *Pronouns* ii. 7, iii. 5, v. 8, viii. 4. אֶתְכֶם for אֶתְכֶן when *ladies* are being addressed.

iv. 2, vi. 6. בָּהֶם ־, ם, of *female sheep*.

vi. 5. הֵם with עֵינַיִךְ.

vi. 8. הֵמָּה, of *queens* and other *ladies*.

The fem. forms כֵן, ־ַךְ, ־ֵן, הֵנָּה הֵן do not appear in this poem. (See Bötticher, *Ausf. Lehrbuch*, 877. 3.) As regards the Verbs the explanation has been given that the Hebrew language has an aversion against the use of the 3rd person plur. fem. imperfect and, apparently, the fem. imperative (*Ges. K.* 145, p. 110, k). Such an explanation, however, would hardly be sufficient to explain the absence of fem. pronouns of the 2nd and 3rd persons plural in so long a work. It would rather seem that this was a peculiarity which passed from popular and vulgar speech, the colloquial speech of common life, into the literary language (see *Ges.-K.* 135 o ; Bötticher, *ubi sup. Del.* p. 46). It may indicate that our poem originated in a district where the distinction between certain masc. and fem. pronominal forms did not prevail, that is, it points to *provincial or*

dialectic variety. Dialects are very often distinguished by violation of
concords about which the standard literary language has developed a
rigidity which did not always exist, and it is reasonable to conclude that
this peculiarity in the use of pronouns is a point in which the dialect of
some country district differed from the Hebrew written in Judæa. In
view of other indications it can hardly be doubted that this was a
Galilean provincialism.

It is true that similar phenomena occur occasionally in other books,
but they never run through a whole book, and where they occur the
masc. pronouns are often intermixed with fem. forms even in the same
sentence, *e.g.* Num. xxvii. 7, Ezek. xxiii. 45, 46, Ruth i. 8, 9. Canticles
however uses them as a matter of course, without any intermixture, even
when *queens* are spoken of. The inference this suggests is that there was
a time when these masc. and fem. forms were not clearly differentiated
and the masc. form served for both genders; and the composition of the
poem would then date from a time when these fem. forms were not
in use, or perhaps from a time when they were extant, but had not been
generally adopted, and the old usage survived in provincial regions. This
view would postulate for our poem *not only a provincial origin, but an
early date.*

(B) Words or forms not found in any other parts of the O.T.
Aramaisms are marked A.

שְׁחַרְחֹרֶת, i. 6. A well-known root and a usual formation, see *Ges.-K.*
84 n.

A. נֹטְרָה, i. 6—8, 11, 12. In the sense of "guarding" (a vineyard).
The same word as נצר (Prov. xxvii. 18 תִּאְצֹר 'נ) with the modification
of spelling ט for צ (Driver, *Tenses*, sec. 178, p. 226), which "shews that the
maid is a Galilean, whose manner of speech is Aramaising, and, if we
may say so, Platt-Hebrew" (*Del.* p. 23).

A. אֵיכָה, i. 7, meaning "where?" 2 Kin. vi. 13 אֵיכֹה. This word
generally means "How!" (Lam. i. 1, iv. 1); it only means "Where?"
in a question in Ephraimite dialect (Bötticher, 530 a).

A. חֲרוּזִים, i. 10.

מֵסַב, i. 12. In sense of "table-banquet." See the verb 1 Sam. xvi. 11.

נֵרְדְּ, i. 12, iv. 13, 14.

כֹּפֶר, i. 14, iv. 13.

A. בְּרוֹתִים, i. 17. Usually בְּרוֹשׁ, the original lisped dental becoming
in Hebrew a simple sibilant (Driver, *ut sup.* 228). An Aramaising
provincialism.

A?. כֹּתֶל, ii. 9. This is usually styled an Aramaism (see Ezra v. 8,
Dan. v. 5) but is really an Assyrian loan-word "*Kutallu*" (Schrader, *Die
Keilins. u. d. A. T.* 2nd ed. p. 457). The Pesh. uses here the word *Ess'tho*,
(see Acts xxiii. 3) and the Targum אֹשׁוּתְנָא. This word does not seem to
be Syriac. It is not in Payne-Smith, *Thes. Syr.*

עֹפֶר, ii. 9, 17, iv. 5, vii. 4, viii. 14.

חָרֵד, ii. 9. The verb Prov. xii. 27.

A. סְתָו, ii. 11. This word is found in the Aramaic inscriptions of Zenjirli (date 747 to 727 B.C.), "בֵּית שְׁתָוָא," "winter house" (Cooke, *North Sem. Ins.* No. 63, l. 18).

נִצָּנִים, ii. 12, from root —נצ"ץ, vi. 11, vii. 13. Comp. the month נִיסָן, Floreal, Es. iii. 7, Neh. ii. 1.

זָמִיר, ii. 12. Comp. זָמִיר, Is. xxv. 5.

A. פַּג, ii. 13.

A. סְמָדַר, ii. 13, 15, vii. 13.

כִּמְעַט שֶׁ...עַד, iii. 4. See Ginsburg *ad loc.*

אַפִּרְיוֹן, iii. 9.

רְפִידָה, iii. 10. See the verb ii. 5.

מְבֻעָר לְ, iv. 1, 3. See Hitzig, *Com.* p. 53.

נֶלְשׁוּ, iv. 1, vi. 5.

מִדְבָּר, iv. 3. (Of the mouth as organ of speech.)

רַחְצָה, iv. 2, vi. 6. Comp. רַחַץ Ps. lx. 10, cviii. 10.

תַּלְפִּיּוֹת, iv. 4.

צִוְּרֹנִים, iv. 9, cognate to צַוָּאר.

שֶׁלַח, iv. 13, in sense of "shoot." Comp. שְׁלֻחֹת, Is. xvi. 8.

כַּרְכֹּם, iv. 14.

A. רְסִיסִים, v. 2.

A. טַף, v. 3, also in Assyrian, Ges.-Buhl Lex. *ad voc.*

תַּלְתַּלִּים, v. 11. Root תלל.

A. קְוֻצּוֹת, v. 2, 11. Root קוץ? Is. xviii. 6. Del. *Com.*

מִלֵּאת, v. 12. See the verb, v. 14.

עָשֶׁת, v. 15. Comp. עָשׂוֹת, Ezek. xxvii. 19.

אֲגֹוֹ, vi. 11.

הֵנֵצוּ, vi. 11, vii. 13. In sense of "bloom." *Ges.-K.* 67. 4 dd, Del. *Com.*

A. אָמָּן, vii. 2. Comp. אָמוֹן, Prov. viii. 30. This word is cognate to Pesh. *Ummonutho* (Acts xix. 24), but is an Assyrian loan-word *Ummanu.* See Brown, *Lex. s.v.*, Schrader-Zimmern, *Die Keil. u. d. A. T.* 3rd ed. 649.

שֻׁרֵּר, vii. 3. Cognate is שֹׁר, Prov. iii. 8, Ez. xvi. 4, Del. *Com.* 123—4.

A. סַהַר, vii. 3. Comp. Targum סִיהֲרָא, vi. 10 and here.

A. מֶזֶג, vii. 3.

A. סוּגָה, Aram. for שׂוּגָה. Hitz. *Com.* p. 88.

סַנְסִנִּים, vii. 9. Compare the proper name סַנְסַנָּה, Jos. xv. 31.

דּוֹבֵב, vii. 10. Probably cognate to דּוּב (Lev. xxvi. 16) and זוּב.

רָקַח, viii. 2. Root רקח.

רָפַק, viii. 5.

(C)   Other provincialisms (Bötticher s. 35).

The uniform use of שֶׁ for אֲשֶׁר.

The paraphrastic genitive as שֶׁלִּי כַּרְמִי, i. 5, viii. 12, see iii. 7.   (König, *Hebr. u. Sem.* Berlin 1901, p. 46.   *Ges.-K.* 135 m, note 3.)

The free use of מִן partitive.

The frequent employment of the ethic dative.

The use of לְ after prepositions and verbs.

Perhaps also the spelling דָּוִיד *plene*, iv. 4.   See Amos vi. 5, ix. 11, Hos. iii. 5.   Ewald, *Dichter* II. 338 n. 1.

רַעְיָה, i. 9, 15 &c. is either archaic or provincial, only found, outside Cant., Jud. xi. 37, but *v.* 38 and Ps. xlv. 15, רֵעָה.

(D)   Other Aramaic words and forms.   (See Bötticher s. 35.   Driver, *Introd.* ed. 8, p. 448.)

מֵעִים for *body*, v. 14.

לֵבָב in the Syrian sense (Pesh. 1 Thess. v. 14), iv. 9.

שַׁלְמָה, see דִּי־לְמָה, Ezra vii. 23, equivalent to דִּי לָא, Dan. ii. 18 (Kautzsch, *Gram. Bib. Aram.* 69. 10).

רָהִיט, i. 17, K'ri, vii. 6.   This is really an Assyrian loan-word *Ratu*. (F. Delitzsch, *Wo lag der Paradies*, p. 143).

הָרְהִיב, vi. 5.   Syr. *Arheb*.

שַׁלְהֶבֶת, viii. 6, apparently from Shaphel of לחב (Del. *Com.* 147).

Asyndeton of narrative verbs as חָלָף הָלַךְ ii. 11, חָמַק עָבַר v. 6.

אֲחוּזֵי, iii. 8, as a deponent.   (See Bötticher 997. γ.)

This language, so plentifully sprinkled with provincial and Aramaic forms, has been happily named by Bötticher (*Lehrbuch*, §§ 29, 34) *Ephraimite*, as signifying that works bearing marks of it shew themselves to have been composed in North Israel.   (See Burney's *Notes on Kings*, pp. 208—9.)

Turning to the Hapaxlegomena enumerated in list B, we notice that the words נֵרְדְּ, כֹּפֶר, כַּרְכֹּם and אֲגוֹז are the names of foreign plants whose names would come with them as *loan-words* when they were introduced into Palestine.   That they were introduced in the time of Solomon is a reasonable inference from his love for botany (1 Kin. v. 13) and from the extensive foreign commerce which grew up in his day.   To whatever foreign language these names may be shewn to belong, when the plants came they would bring their names with them, as certainly happened in other cases. "When Solomon's ships brought him the peacocks, apes, ivory, almug or algum wood, they brought with them also the Sanskrit and Malabar names of the ape and of the algum wood, the Tamul name of the peacock and the Sanskrit of the elephant" (Pusey, *Lect. on Daniel*, 9th ed. p. 26). These plant-names in all probability came in a similar way.   It is also extremely likely that אַפִּרְיוֹן as a Sanskrit loan-word (see Hitzig, *Com.*; Brown, *Lex. s.v.*) came in the same way, name and thing together.

Passing over for a moment the Aramaic words and forms, it is curious to notice that most of the other words in list B are derived from or related to well-known Hebrew roots and forms, and that many of them only differ slightly in formation or sound from words which are extant in other parts of Hebrew literature. The inference can hardly be resisted that they are dialectic variations from the literary language, in fact *provincialisms*. The peculiarities of provincial speech are usually found to be either differences in the forms of words, or variations in pronunciation from standard literary forms, and these are just the phenomena we find here. The question now arises whether it is possible that Canticles, written in this peculiar dialect, full of Aramaic and provincial words and forms, and foreign loan-words, can have originated at the early period which on general grounds seems most suitable for its composition ; or must it be ascribed, as many writers of late are disposed to think, to those post-exilic days, in which Aramaic gradually invaded the pure Hebrew written in Judah, "until at last, somewhere about the middle of the second century B.C., Aramean became the general country speech in Syria, Palestine and the lands on their Eastern boundaries" (Kautzsch, *Gram. Bib. Aram.* p. 2)? Such writers would classify Canticles with Eccl. and Chronicles rather than with Judges v.

In these discussions much stress is laid on the exclusive use in Cant. of שׁ relativum, also as conjunction (Budde, p. xxiv); it will therefore be desirable to examine the use of this particle. The first instance of its appearance in Hebrew literature (omitting, as too uncertain, Gen. vi. 3 and xlix. 10) is in the Song of Deborah, Jud. v., a piece whose authenticity is undoubted (Wellhausen, *Gesch.* Aufl. v. p. 11). Verse 7 has twice שַׁקַּמְתִּי. The next three instances occur in the history of Gideon, and (it will be observed) in the older narrative, which was fitted into his framework by the Deuteronomic editor (Driver, *Introd.* ed. I. 157). These are some of the oldest narratives in the O.T.; they ignore Judah, and view the time of the Judges as the preparation for the Ephraimite kingdom (Wellhausen, *Comp.* 3rd Aufl. 215, 233); they were certainly written in North Israel. The instances are Jud. vi. 17 שָׁאַתָּה, vii. 12 שֶׁעַל, viii. 26 *ib.* Budde (*u.s.*) disposes of these instances in Judges in two ways: first, they are all *glosses*; secondly, the books were not subjected to the revision of learned men. These reasons are mutually destructive. If the instances are glosses they must have been put in by editors ; if editors did not revise the books, we have the original text.

The next instance is 2 Kings vi. 11 מִשֶּׁלָּנוּ occurring in an episode of the history of Elisha attributed to a Samaritan collection of prophetic histories originating not long after 760 B.C. (Kittel, *Gesch. des V. I.* Bd 2, 2nd Aufl. 286). To these instances may be added the (somewhat doubtful) evidence of a weight found on the site of Samaria with an inscription in

characters of the eighth century, said to contain the form שֶׁל used
genitivally as in Cant. iii. 7. (Driver, *Introd.* ed. I. 422, ed. VIII. 449.
Sayce, *Higher Criticism* &c., p. 449.)
From this point (with the exception of the instances in Cant.) the
form disappears from Heb. literature for centuries. It reappears in Post-
exilic books (Lam., Eccl., Jonah, some late Psalms, Ezra, Chron.) as a part
of the Aramaic which was gradually becoming the current speech of the
Hebrew people. These facts are enough to shew that a document *need*
not be post-exilic in date simply because it uses שֶׁ for אֲשֶׁר, that it may on
the other hand be earlier than 760 B.C., and that, if otherwise appearing
to be Ephraimite, it is more likely to be of the earlier date.

Some further light may be obtained on this subject by observing the
presence of this particle in early Aramean inscriptions. In two such
inscriptions found in 1891 at Merab near Aleppo (Cooke, *North Sem. Inscr.*
Nos. 64 and 65) (see No. 39) שֶׁ appears, used much as שֶׁל in Heb. and ד in
later Aramaic, to express the genitival relation. No. 64 is the epitaph of
a local priest, and the first word is שְׁשִׂנזרבן "(the tomb) of Sinzirban."
"This שֶׁ must be a relative and sign of the genitive" (Cooke, *ad loc.*).
Similarly No. 65, first word שְׁאַגבר "(the tomb) of Agbar," another local
priest. These inscriptions are assigned to the 7th cent. B.C. and are
therefore later than the Heb. instances quoted above. Apparently the
reason that שֶׁ in North Israel disappeared and made way for אֲשֶׁר was the
influence of the Phoenician language. The Phoenician relative pronoun
was אֵשׁ pronounced as a monosyllable *ish* or *ash*. "The etymology of אֵשׁ is
obscure. Taking שֶׁ as the original element, it is possible that א, properly
a demonstrative sound (Deutelaut), was added to it....Whatever the relation
between אֵשׁ and אֲשֶׁר may be, in actual usage the Phoen. אֵשׁ forms
historically a link between the Heb. שֶׁ and אֲשֶׁר" (Cooke, p. 20, and to the
same effect König, *Lehrgeb.* II. 323). The latter writer states that the
existence of שֶׁ as a mere *să*, *sĕ* is absolutely assured, and considers
unlikely the suggestion (see Graetz, *Shir-ha-Shirim* 44) that the Phoenicians
shortened אֲשֶׁר at the same period as the Hebrews (*op. cit.* 325). Such
a view as that of Graetz is now quite untenable in view of the evidence of
the inscriptions. König is also of the very likely opinion that the forms
שֶׁ, אֵשׁ and אֲשֶׁר may have existed side by side in different dialects or forms
of speech or in various parts of the country for a long period.

This view of the position harmonises all the facts, the appearance of שֶׁ
in Ephraimite writings all before or in the 8th century B.C., its disappear-
ance from Hebrew literature after that date—its continuance in Aramean—
and its reappearance in Hebrew literature as Aramean gradually reintro-
duced itself into that literature in post-exilic times.

It seems clear then that the use of שֶׁ in Canticles does not prove
lateness of composition, but it is suggested that the *exclusive* use of שֶׁ
does. Now it is somewhat singular that there is no late book in which

this particle is used exclusively. Even in the admittedly late, almost Mishnic, Hebrew of *Eccl.*, שֶׁ occurs 68 times, and אֲשֶׁר preponderates, being used 89 times. So in other late books. In *Jonah* שֶׁ is used 4 times and אֲשֶׁר 9 times. *Lamentations* has שֶׁ 4 times. *Ezra* 3 times. All the late books which use שֶׁ use אֲשֶׁר as well, and apparently on no principle or rule which can be discerned. Canticles differs from them all in using it exclusively. It is only in the title, which is later than the book, that אֲשֶׁר is used. This latter fact is very significant. The title was probably added in the middle period of the language, when the use of שֶׁ had disappeared from literary style altogether. The editor, whoever he was, found שֶׁ written throughout the book, but that particle had gone out of use in his day, it was an archaism, so he used in his superscription the form אֲשֶׁר to which he was accustomed. If he had added the title to the poem at a very late date, say the date of Eccl. or later, the use of שֶׁ would have been current, and finding it used throughout the poem he would certainly have written it in his title.

Viewed in the light of these phenomena the argument of late date from the *exclusive* use of שֶׁ proves too much. If it is a proof of late date, it suggests a date far later than Eccl., so late that it would be impossible to understand how the book was ever received into the Hebrew Canon (see sec. 14 *sup.*). Being an isolated phenomenon in O.T. literature, it suggests, rather, *provincial peculiarity.*

We conclude, on the whole, that the use of שֶׁ in this poem cannot be adduced as a proof of late date. It is compatible with an early date. The result of the evidence cannot be better stated than in the careful phrase of Driver (*Genesis* p. 412), "It (שֶׁ) occurs peculiarly, and only in books or passages which were either, it seems, written in N. Palestine, *or* are late."

It remains to consider the general question whether the Aramaisms in Canticles necessarily imply a post-exilic date, and in dealing with this subject, the geographical situation of Syria and its historic relations with Israel cannot be overlooked. That Israel had Aramaic origins is clearly shewn by the stories of the Patriarchs (see especially Gen. xxiv. xxvii.—xxxi.), and that this fact was clearly impressed upon the national consciousness appears from Deut. xxvi. 5, אֲרַמִּי אֹבֵד אָבִי. And when the tribes of Israel had settled in Palestine, Aram bordered them on the North and East. Further than this, David had conquered and annexed to his realm the whole of Aram as far as the Euphrates, and Damascus was tributary to him and received his governors (2 Sam. viii. 6, see Cant. vii. 5). These double relations of vicinity and conquest must have led to a lively intercourse between the Northern tribes and the Syrians, and the wars between the two after the disruption kept the rival nations in contact with one another (see *e.g.* 2 Kings cc. v.—viii.). The trade relations of Israel which grew up in the time of Solomon must have proved a strong reason for mutual intercourse between the two peoples. The trade route from

Damascus to the Sea by necessity ran through Israelite territory. "It would run from Damascus in a southerly direction to the neighbourhood of the Sea of Galilee, would cross the Jordan at this point, and turn through the territory of Zabulon and Naphthali towards Akko" (Kittel, *Gesch.*, 2nd Aufl. Bd II. 223). Nor must it be forgotten that, in the time of Ahab, Israelite merchants had bazaars in Damascus and Syrians in Samaria (1 Kin. xx. 34).

It is impossible to conceive that all these circumstances in combination, identity of origins, geographical proximity, wars, incorporation by conquest, trade relations, could have remained without effect on the spoken language of the Northern tribes of Israel. What this effect was, has been well stated by Renan. "On doit supposer que les tribus du Nord, *voisines de Syrie*, parlaient dès le temps du royaume d'Israël un dialecte plus rapproché de l'araméen....Il faut donc s'en tenir à ce fait, qu'au dessous de la langue régulière, qui seule nous a été transmise, il existait une langue populaire, sentant le patois, chargée de provincialismes, et variable suivant les cantons. *Dialecte* et *incorrection* sont deux idées bien voisines ...le mot même dialecte designait à son origine le langage usuel, par opposition au langage écrit....Un autre fait, non moins digne de remarque, c'est l'analogie frappant qu'ont tous ces irrégularités provinciales avec l'araméen. Il semble que, même avant la captivité, le patois populaire se rapprochait beaucoup de cette langue, en sorte qu'il nous est maintenant impossible de séparer bien nettement dans le style de certains écrits, ce qui appartient au dialecte populaire, ou au patois de royaume d'Israël, ou à l'influence des temps de la captivité" (*Hist. des langues sémitiques*, 5th ed. 142—3). To the same effect Bötticher observes, "Andres ist zugleich in Aramäischen gebräuchlich gewesen, also der Nähe Syrien's wegen dem Nord-hebräischen theils von jeher mit jenem gemein gewesen, theils doch früher als dem Judäischen geflossen. Darum *trifft das Ephraimitische in Vielem mit dem jüngern Hebräism überein, ohne deshalb ihn anzugehören*, und für die (Cant.) einen späteren Ursprung zu bewiesen" (*Lehrbuch*, 35).

Such would seem to be a sound view of the facts. Aramaisms in a Heb. document may be consistent with an early date or with a late date. They may have flowed from the common origin and close association of Syrians and N. Israelites, or they may have resulted from the forces which introduced Aramaic into Palestine after the exile. From *which* period their occurrence in a book is to be dated must be decided by an examination of all the criteria.

One of such criteria is found in the fact that the Aramaisms of Cant. have a character of their own. They are nearly all ἅπαξ λεγόμενα and some of them are demonstrably of early date. One סְתָיו we have seen to be Old Aramean, extant *cir.* 740 B.C. Three words, commonly styled Aramean, כֹּתֶל, אַפִּן, and רָהִים (and probably several others), are really Assyrian loan-words (see אֲנָ Schrader, *Die K. I. u. d. A. T.* 3rd ed. 649), and generally the Aramaisms of Cant. are peculiar to the book, and have

little affinity to those found in late books. For example, the "list of
Hapaxlegomena and of the words and forms in Koheleth belonging to
a more recent period of the language" in Delitzsch's *Com.* 1891, p. 190 fol.,
contains 95 items, of which *only two* שׁ and פַּרְדֵּס appear in Cant.
Similarly in the very close and full analysis of the language of Eccl. in
Siegfried's *Com.* pp. 13—23, *one parallel* is quoted from Cant., viz. שׁוּק
(Street), also in Prov. vii. 8, and *one contrast*, the later plur. מַעֲנוֹת as
against מַעֲנוּגִים, Cant. vii. 7. With these exceptions none of the late
Hebrew words noted by Siegfried in Eccl. and *not one* of his Aramaisms
or Graecisms appear in Cant. In the list of 46 linguistic peculiarities
of *Chron.* given by Driver (*Int.*) no parallel is found in Cant.; and the
Aramaisms of *Jonah*, and the words or idioms peculiar to *Esther* noted
by the same writer are also entirely absent. In view of these facts it
is not too much to say that, compared with post-exilic books, this poem
has an Aramaic vocabulary which is almost entirely its own. Its language
is *sui generis*. Cant. is in fact an isolated phenomenon in O.T. literature.
Nothing at all like it is extant. There is therefore no standard of
comparison to which we may refer its diction. Many of its peculiarities
are without parallels in any other book. Its *exclusive use* of certain masc.
pronouns, and of שׁ, its long list of Hebrew words and forms found nowhere
else, the usages we have called "provincialisms," its array of Aramaic
words used nowhere else in the O.T., its loan-words, these features stamp
the diction as unique also. This Hebrew is not the Hebrew of Chron.
still less of Eccl., it is something quite different, and the matter is perhaps
understated by Driver (*Introd.* 8th ed., p. 475), who affirms that the
linguistic peculiarities of Cant. treated as dialectical usages seem in most
cases to be compatible with an early date.

We regard as entirely unfounded the assumption of Graetz and others,
that because certain words appear only in Cant. and in late (Mishnic)
Heb., therefore Cant. must have been written at a late date. The true
inference from these facts is all the other way. The very peculiar diction
of Cant., containing so large a number of words not appearing in any other
extant remains of classical Heb., must have been an object of great
interest in later times; and as some of these words are *proved* to be old,
and all *may* be, it is almost certain that their appearance in late Heb.
writings is due to their being taken from Cant. or perhaps from lost
secular poems of a similar character. The songs sung at feasts (Am. vi. 5,
Is. v. 12, xxiv. 9) as well as Solomon's collection (1 Kin. v. 11) are hopelessly
lost to us. Had some of these escaped the ravages of time it is possible
that the list of ἅπαξ λεγ. in Canticles might have been a shorter one.

Although the language of Canticles has been shown to be by no means
incompatible with an early date, there is one word, פַּרְדֵּס iv. 13, which
has been thought to bring its composition down as far as the Persian
period, *circ.* 500 B.C. As this is not in itself a likely date (although it is

that of König, *Einleit.* 423), this word should be carefully examined. It is well known in its Greek form παράδεισος, which denoted "walled enclosures of a large size, well wooded, and watered with sparkling streams in which were bred or kept wild beasts of various kinds, chiefly of the more harmless sorts, as stags and antelopes and wild sheep. These the kings pursued and shot with arrows, or brought down with the javelin" (Rawlinson, *Monarchies* III. 228). These *paradises* were frequently of great extent; thus Cyrus on one occasion reviewed the Greek army in his paradise, and on another occasion the Greeks were alarmed by a report that there was a great army in a neighbouring paradise. (Xenophon, *Anab.*, quoted Smith, *Dict. Ant.* 2nd ed. *s.v.*) Now a hunting park of this kind is quite suitable to the use of the word פַּרְדֵּס in Neh. ii. 8 and in Eccl. ii. 5, but is most unsuitable as applied to a clump of pomegranate trees in Cant. iv. 13. And this is probably the reason why the LXX. translator, not being able to make sense of the expression "a hunting park of pomegranates," left out the word ῥοῶν altogether. (See Exc. I *sup.*) The difficulty was a real one. If פַּרְדֵּס here is the same word and means the same thing as the παράδεισος of Xenophon, the phrase פַּרְדֵּס רִמּוֹנִים is unintelligible.

There is much uncertainty about this word. The Greeks seem to have taken it from the Persians, but whether it is originally Iranian has been doubted. Commentators generally, following Delitzsch, have derived it from the Zend *pairi-daeza* which is stated to occur once in the Vendidad, but this derivation has been disputed. It is difficult for any one entirely unacquainted with Zend fully to appreciate the discussions on this subject. What follows is taken from those who are qualified to speak on the matter. (See Lagarde, *Gesammelte Abhand.* pp. 76, 211; Boetticher 38; Fried. Delitzsch, *Wo lag der Paradies*, 95 fol.; Bruston, *La Sulammite*, p. 50.) It is stated that :

1. The derivation of פרדם from this Zend word is doubted on various grounds. The word is thought rather to be derived from or through Armenian. It only appears once in the Vendidad, and nowhere else, and has left no trace in modern Persian but is extant in Armenian (*pardez*).

2. The word in the Vendidad appears to mean nothing more than "the act of building a heap or wall round something" but not "the place enclosed within the wall or heap," much less "a garden": on the other hand the Armenian *pardez* does mean "a garden."

In view of these uncertainties, the difference between the meaning of the word in Neh. and Eccl. and in Cant. is very striking. In Neh. ii. 8 it denotes a *park* so spacious that it would be a simple matter to cut sufficient timber in it to repair all the fortifications of Jerusalem. So also in Eccl. ii. 5, among the great works of a wise and powerful king are enumerated גַּנּוֹת וּפַרְדֵּסִים, suitably rendered by the LXX. κήπους καὶ παραδείσους, gardens *and hunting parks*. But in Cant. iv. 13 the meaning is very different: it is a *bed or shrubbery* in a garden. The sense of the passage is, " *Thou art* (like) *a locked garden, and what grows in thee* (שְׁלָחַיִךְ) *is* (like) *a clump of pomegranates,*" with a long enumeration of other fruits and flowers. The word פַּרְדֵּם here does not mean as much as a *garden,* only a part of that which grows in a garden.

This wide difference in the meaning of this word argues a long interval between the dates of the composition of the documents. If Cant. had been written in the Perso-Greek period the author *could not* have written פַּרְדֵּם παράδεισος, which meant and was well known to mean a *royal hunting park,* to denote *a group of fruit trees.* It can only be concluded from the facts that this word had entered the language, as a loan-word, in some such sense as a *garden bed,* at some period considerably anterior to the Persian era. Such a conclusion is quite reasonable in the present state of knowledge. It is now well known from the Boghaz-Köi tablets that Aryan-speaking people were living in Asia Minor about 1500 B.C., and the Amarna tablets have revealed a number of Aryan words in Syria and Palestine about the same period. It is clear that at this period a wave of Aryan population passed over Syria (Kittel, *Gesch.* Bd I., 2nd Aufl., 1912, pp. 45, 83, 630). It is now almost universally admitted that the primitive seats of the Aryans were in Europe and that the migration of the Indo-Iranians was eastward (Taylor, *Origin of the Aryans,* pp. 52—3). It is thought that it was in some stage of this mighty wandering that they touched Palestine and left there traces of their language and other signs of their presence (Kittel, *u.s.*). If this be so, and if our poem, which in its vocabulary contains nothing else which is not compatible with an early date, contains a supposed Iranian loan-word, there is no difficulty in assuming that this word was left by the Iranians as they sojourned in Syro-Palestine in their long march to their Eastern goal.

It is worthy of note that the LXX. in some places use παράδεισος as the equivalent of גַן, and always where it is intended to give the sense of a *wide and spacious extent of country.* Thus in Gen. ii. 8 (see v. 15, iii. 24) it denotes a park, containing every kind of tree, watered by a river, and in which was found every kind of animal, an ideal Persian *paradise.* In Gen. xiii. 10 it is the whole of the *kikkar,* as well watered as Yahveh's garden, alluding to ii. 8. In Num. xxiv. 6 it is the widespread encampment of Israel by the river as seen from a mountain height. See also Joel ii. 3 (the whole land), Is. li. 3 (the steppes), Ezek. xxxi. 8, 9 (a park with cedars, cypresses, and other trees). If the Greek word had this sense at the period of translation, it is not surprising that the LXX. translators of the Song were puzzled about the sense, and altered the text to make it less incongruous.

On the whole, the doubts and uncertainties which surround this word are such that it cannot be regarded as any criterion of date.

EXCURSUS IV

QUOTATIONS FROM THE SONG IN OTHER BOOKS

(a) Hosea.

In the passage Hosea xiv. 6—9, there are no less than 7 supposed verbal parallels to expressions found in Cant. These are as follows :

(a) Hos. כַּשּׁוֹשַׁנָּה.   Cant. ii. 2 כְּשׁוֹשַׁנָּה.

The fem. form of this word occurs nowhere else outside Cant. except 2 Chr. iv. 5 without the article.

(b) Hos. כַּלְּבָנוֹן.   Cant. v. 15 כַּלְּבָנוֹן.

Lebanon is only mentioned in Hos. in this passage where it occurs 3 times.

(c) Hos. וְרֵיחַ לוֹ כַּלְּבָנוֹן.   Cant. iv. 11 כְּרֵיחַ לְבָנוֹן.

A very striking parallel.

(d) Hos. יֹשְׁבֵי בְצִלּוֹ, or better as corrected by LXX. &c. וְיָשֻׁבוּ (Harper, *Structure Hosea*, p. 50 n. 151).   Cant. ii. 3 בְּצִלּוֹ...וְיָשַׁבְתִּי.

This combination of words does not otherwise occur till later than Hos. See Ezek. xxxi. 6, 17.

(e) Hos. וְיִפְרְחוּ כַגָּפֶן.   Cant. vi. 11, vii. 13 הֵפְרְחָה הַגֶּפֶן.

פרח is a common word (see Hos. x. 4), but this combination does not occur anywhere else.

(f) Hos. כִּבְרוֹשׁ רַעֲנָן.   Cant. i. 17 בְּרוֹתִים, i. 16 רַעֲנָנָה.

Neither word is uncommon, but neither otherwise occurs in Hos., and the occurrences in Cant. are close together.

(g) Hos. פֶּרְיְךָ.   Cant. ii. 3 פִּרְיוֹ.

Too common a word to amount to much.

The combined effect of at any rate the first six of these coincidences is very striking, especially when it is borne in mind that they all occur in three verses of Hosea. One of these writers must have read the other, and it is hardly possible that Cant. should have borrowed these expressions from Hosea. They are all contained in one short passage in Hosea, whereas in Cant. they are scattered all over the book, one of them (e) occurs in two places, and they not only belong, so to speak, more to the texture of the work, but are certainly used in it in too original and characteristic a manner to be mere echoes of the slight use in Hosea. The *lily* (a) and *Lebanon* (b) and (c) are prominent features throughout Cant.; the heroine is "a lily," and Lebanon with its cedars and its waterfalls is very prominent throughout. The *sitting in the shade* of the beloved (d), and the *blossoming of vines* (*e*), are more than mere rhetorical terms; they take an important place in the development of the action: they have not the appearance of being copied phrases, but spring naturally into being in the situation where they are found. In Hosea on the other hand they have every appearance of being borrowed, they are simply used as similes, without any relation to each other, and it is not in every case clear what their exact force is meant to be. How much less pointed and clear, *e.g.*, is the reference to those who will *again sit under his shade* (*d*), than the use of the same phrase in Cant.

It is indeed the use of these borrowed phrases which gives this passage its peculiar colour, and which may serve to explain why it so markedly differs from the rest of Hosea. The second portion of this book, c. iv.–xiv., "has the appearance of having been compiled by the author out of utterances and fragments of discourses which orally had been delivered by him at different times throughout the remainder of his long ministry" (Huxtable in *Speaker's Com.*). Thus xiv. 1(Heb. 2)—9 may be regarded as a separate oracle or discourse, and *vv.* 6—9 as a separate fragment or section of that discourse. In view of the phenomena above set out, it is not unreasonable to assume that the prophet shortly before the composition of this particular oracle (or of this section of it) had heard the Song read or recited. Some of its most striking phrases had struck him and remained in his memory.

The frequent mention of *lilies*, and the striking prominence given to *Lebanon*, are salient features which would impress any reader. The *scent of Lebanon—I sat in his shade* with delight—the *blossoming of the vine*— the *cypresses* arching over nature's *green* divan, were phrases well calculated to catch the attention of one who was himself a master of style. It is the poet who can best appreciate the poet. So then, when he is setting himself to deliver this oracle of comfort, not only do these phrases remain in his memory and fall from his lips, but his whole speech reflects something of the brightness and joy in nature which breathe through the Song. This passage has all the colour of Galilee, with Lebanon in the distance, its mighty roots, its wine, its scent. Like the Song, this oracle "is saturated with the fragrant atmosphere of the Northern mountains" (Adeney in *Expos. Bible*). It is not that the prophet consciously quotes, but that the phrases of the Song have become at this time part of his mental atmosphere, and flow without effort into his discourse.

If this be so, some light may be thrown on the difficulty which has been felt as to the presence of this oracle in the works of Hosea. It has been the opinion of many modern expositors that xiv. 1—9 is not the work of Hosea, but that, with other passages, it is a Messianic insertion of a time following Ezekiel and Deutero-Isaiah which entirely changed the function and character of his book. (See W. R. Harper, *Int. crit. Com. Amos and Hosea*, p. clix. and 408—9. Contra, G. A. Smith, *Exp. Bible, Hosea*. See also Davidson, Hastings' *Dict.*, s.v. *Hosea*.) The writer does not take this view: he sees no reason why a promise of restored prosperity following on repentance and amendment should be unnatural in this Ephraimitic prophet. Nor is there in the piece anything specifically Messianic—much less Judaic—and the tone and colouring of the passage are most distinctly North Israelite. The only importance of this question to the present discussion is the *date* at which the literary influence of the Song reveals itself in other literature. If Hosea wrote this oracle, the Song is quoted before 735 B.C. If on the other hand it is of the period of Deut.-Isaiah or later, this would bring down the date of quotation to about 500 B.C. In either case the fact of quotation or reference renders it impossible to ascribe the poem to the Greek period, a conclusion to which we have already been led by other reasons (Excursus I, *sup.*).

(b) PROVERBS.

Most striking parallels occur between certain portions of the Introduction to Proverbs, cc. 1—9, and Cant., and, singularly enough, they are all to be found in those passages, Prov. v., vi. 20—35, vii., which deal with fidelity to the marriage tie and warnings against adultery.

The most important of these is Prov. vi. 31 אֶת־כָּל־הוֹן בֵּיתוֹ יִתֵּן compared with אִם־יִתֵּן אִישׁ אֶת־כָּל־הוֹן בֵּיתוֹ Cant. viii. 7.

It can hardly be doubted, not only that this a direct quotation by one from the other, but that the passage in Cant. is the original. It is a powerful apposite phrase to say in reference to a king, *If he would give all the wealth of his house* for love, men would despise him. But to say, as Proverbs does, that a thief who steals to satisfy his hunger, if he is caught, will have to repay sevenfold, *he must give all the wealth of his house*, is very poor and inappropriate. How much wealth is there likely to be in the house of one who steals through hunger? The author is evidently quoting a familiar phrase. (The unobtrusive link יָבוּז, Prov. vi. 29, Cant. viii. 7 should be noticed.)

In view of this case we shall not have much difficulty in coming to the conclusion that Prov. v. 3 נֹפֶת תִּטֹּפְנָה שִׂפְתֵי זָרָה is a direct quotation from נֹפֶת תִּטֹּפְנָה שִׂפְתוֹתַיִךְ, Cant. iv. 11.

The remaining places are rather reminiscences than direct quotations.

In Prov. v. 15—17 occur וְנֹזְלִים (see also Jer. xviii. 14), בְּאֵרֶךְ, מַעְיְנֹתֶיךָ, all which occur in one verse, Cant. iv. 15.

In Prov. vii. 17 מֹר אֲהָלִים וְקִנָּמוֹן remind us of וְקִנָּמוֹן and מֹר וַאֲהָלוֹת, Cant. iv. 14. The word קנמון occurs nowhere else, except in construct state Ex. xxx. 23. In Ps. xlv. 9 in a somewhat similar phrase קְצִיעוֹת is used.

A review of these facts makes it practically certain that the author of Prov. i.—ix. had read the Song. And so apparently had the author of the

piece Prov. xxxi. 10—31. Verse 28, קָמוּ בָנֶיהָ וַיְאַשְּׁרוּהָ בַּעְלָהּ וַיְהַלְלָהּ, seems to
be a plain quotation of רָאוּהָ בָנוֹת וַיְאַשְּׁרוּהָ מְלָכוֹת וּפִילַגְשִׁים וַיְהַלְלוּהָ, Cant.
vi. 9.

Here again the passage in Cant. is far more natural and appropriate
than that in Proverbs. The *girls* of the Harem naturally *called* the
Shulamite *lucky* on account of her beauty, just as Leah was sure that
other *girls would call her lucky*, because she had so many sons (Gen. xxx.
13). But it is not very suitable that the *sons* of the model housewife
should *call her lucky*, because she practised all the domestic virtues. The
phrase here is quoted, rather than original.

The date of the completed Book of Proverbs is now considered to be
the 4th or 3rd century B.C. (Toy in *Enc. Bib.* art. "Proverbs." See also
W. Nowack in Hastings' *Dict.*). We may take the phenomena above
described as evidence of the literary use of the Song *cir.* 300 B.C.

INDEX

For EU product safety concerns, contact us at Calle de José Abascal, 56–1°,
28003 Madrid, Spain or eugpsr@cambridge.org.

www.ingramcontent.com/pod-product-compliance
Ingram Content Group UK Ltd.
Pitfield, Milton Keynes, MK11 3LW, UK
UKHW040616240426
470322UK00010B/152